COLLI...

DUBLIN
STREETFINDER
COLOUR ATLAS & GUIDE

CONTENTS

2 - 3	Dublin Route Planning Map
4 - 7	Dublin Area Map
8 - 17	Dublin City Guide
18 - 19	Key to Map Pages
20 - 63	Main Maps
64 - 80	Index to Street Names

LEGEND

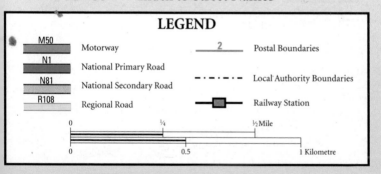

M50 Motorway		**2** Postal Boundaries	
N1 National Primary Road		– · – · – Local Authority Boundaries	
N81 National Secondary Road		▬▬■▬▬ Railway Station	
R108 Regional Road			

```
0              ¼              ½ Mile
|—————————————————————————————————|
0                   0.5              1 Kilometre
```

...shed by Collins
...print of HarperCollinsPublishers
... Fulham Palace Road, Hammersmith, London W6 8JB

...arperCollins website address is: www.**fire**and**water**.com

...right © HarperCollinsPublishers Ltd 1999   Mapping © Bartholomew Ltd. 1988, 1990, 1992, 1993, 1996, 1997, 1998, 1999

...s® is a registered trade mark of HarperCollinsPublishers Limited

...d upon Ordnance Survey Ireland with the permission of the Government © Government of Ireland

...d in Great Britain   ISBN 0 00 448871 7   MI10193   BNN   e-mail: roadcheck@harpercollins.co.uk

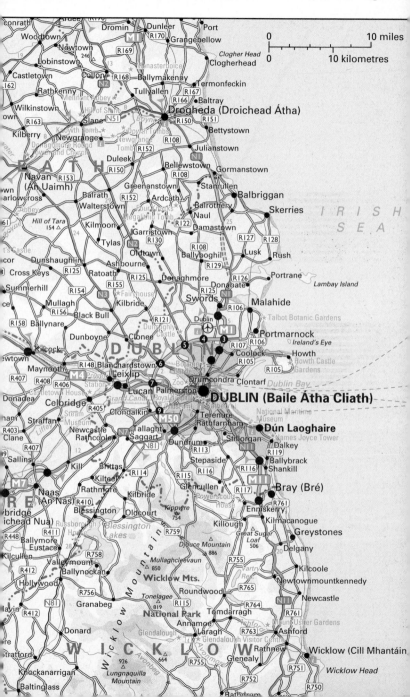

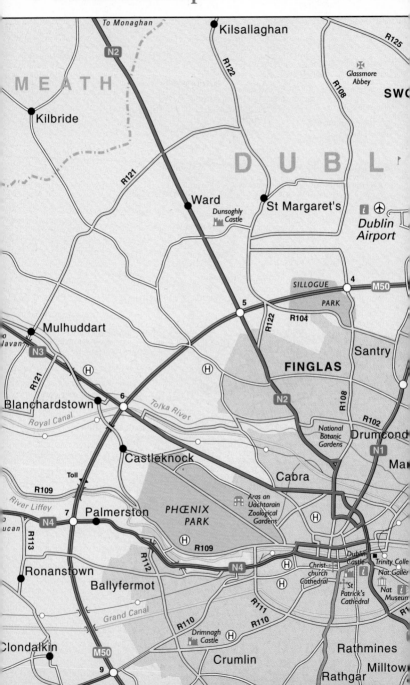

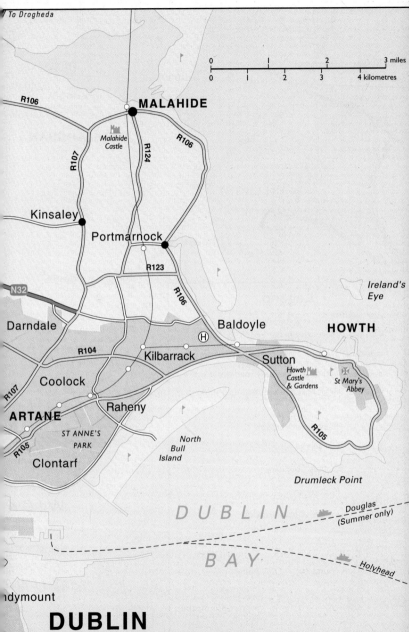

To Drogheda

R106

MALAHIDE

Malahide Castle

R107

R124

R106

Kinsaley

Portmarnock

R123

R106

N32

Darndale

Baldoyle

HOWTH

Ireland's Eye

R104

Kilbarrack

Sutton

Howth Castle & Gardens

St Mary's Abbey

R107

Coolock

R105

Raheny

ARTANE

ST ANNE'S PARK

North Bull Island

R105

Clontarf

R105

Drumleck Point

DUBLIN

Douglas (Summer only)

BAY

Holyhead

dymount

DUBLIN
BAILE ÁTHA CLIATH

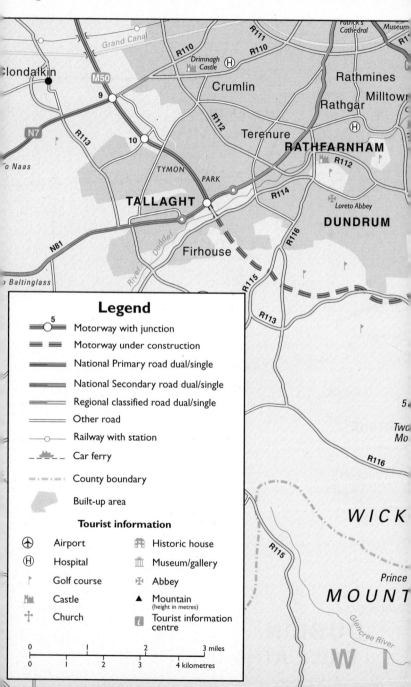

Patrick's Cathedral
Museum

R111
R110
R110
Grand Canal
Clondalkin
M50
9
Drimnagh Castle (H)
Rathmines
Crumlin
Milltown
Rathgar
N7
R113
10
Terenure
(H)
R112
RATHFARNHAM
To Naas
TYMON
PARK
R112
TALLAGHT
R114
Loreto Abbey
DUNDRUM
N81
River Dodder
Firhouse
R116
R115
R113
R115
R116
5

Two
Mo

WICK

Prince

MOUNT

Glencree River

W   I

Legend

═○═ 5	Motorway with junction
▬ ▬	Motorway under construction
▬▬▬	National Primary road dual/single
▬▬	National Secondary road dual/single
══	Regional classified road dual/single
═══	Other road
─○─	Railway with station
_▬_	Car ferry
▪ ▪ ▪	County boundary
◈	Built-up area

Tourist information

⊕	Airport	🏠	Historic house
Ⓗ	Hospital	🏛	Museum/gallery
⚑	Golf course	✠	Abbey
🏰	Castle	▲	Mountain (height in metres)
✝	Church	i	Tourist information centre

0	1	2	3 miles
0	1	2	3	4 kilometres

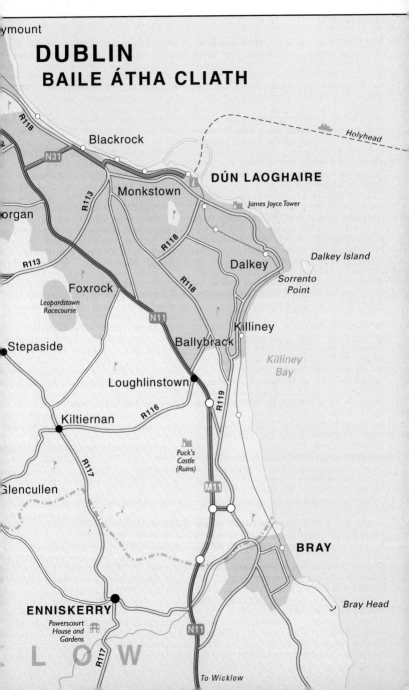

ymount

DUBLIN
BAILE ÁTHA CLIATH

R118

Blackrock

N31

DÚN LAOGHAIRE

Holyhead

Monkstown

R113

James Joyce Tower

organ

R118

R113

Dalkey

Dalkey Island

Foxrock

R118

Sorrento
Point

Leopardstown
Racecourse

N11

Killiney

Stepaside

Ballybrack

Killiney
Bay

Loughlinstown

R116

R119

Kiltiernan

Puck's
Castle
(Ruins)

R117

M11

Glencullen

BRAY

Bray Head

ENNISKERRY

Powerscourt
House and
Gardens

N11

L O W

R117

To Wicklow

HISTORY

The ford over the River Liffey has been important since Celtic times, and there was a thriving Christian community here from the 5thC, following their conversion by St Patrick in AD448. In AD840 the marauding Vikings landed here, built a fortress on the high ground and established a settlement along the banks of the estuary. Originally a base for their numerous raiding sorties, it soon became a flourishing trading port as well, but Viking dominance was severely curtailed following a defeat by Brian Boru at the Battle of Clontarf in 1014.

Converted by Christianity, the Vikings were finally driven out by the Anglo-Normans under Strongbow, who took Dublin by storm, executing the Viking leader, Hasculf. In 1172 Henry II, having established his feudal rights over the invading force, received the submission of the Irish chieftains on the site of College Green. He granted the city by charter to the men of Bristol, from whence the Anglo-Normans had originally come.

The city and surrounding area, established as the seat of English government and protected by an enclosing wall and strategic castles, was known as The Pale. Frequently attacked during the 12thC and 13thC by the Irish clans based in the Wicklow Mountains, it was assaulted unsuccessfully by Edward Bruce in 1316. The city witnessed the crowning of Lambert Simnel, pretender to the English throne, in Christ Church in 1486. Unmoved by the rebellion of 'Silken' Thomas Fitzgerald in 1534, the inhabitants remained loyal to the English crown, supporting King Charles during the Civil Wars. Captured by the Parliamentarians in 1647, the city underwent a great architectural expansion following the Restoration of Charles II. During the Williamite wars Dublin was a Jacobite stronghold. It was here that James II held his last parliament in 1689.

By the end of the 17thC, Dublin was already a flourishing commercial centre; public street lighting had been introduced in 1697 and during the following century the city was transformed into one of the handsomest of Georgian cities. The 'Wide Streets Commission' was established in 1757 and in 1773 the Paving Board was formed. New, elegantly spacious streets and squares

were planned and palatial town hou built. In 1783 the Irish Parliament v granted a short-lived autonomy but th was growing political unrest, wh erupted in the uprising of 1798. L Edward Fitzgerald died of woun sustained resisting arrest and in 1800 detested Act of Union was establish and the fortunes of the city began wane.

With government now in London, few the noblemen required their f mansions and many returned to th country estates or left for Lond Bitterness increased; in 1803 the L Chief Justice was assassinated and Rob Emmet, the leader of an abort insurrection, was hanged. The newspa *The Nation* was established by Char Gavan Duffy in 1842, the heyday of Repeal Movement. In 1841 Dar O'Connell was elected Lord Mayor; o three years later he was interned Richmond Gaol for campaigning for repeal of the Union and the restoration Grattan's 'Irish Parliament'. In 1873 first great Home Rule Conference v held. In 1879 the Land League v formed, whose leaders, including Parr and Davitt, were imprisoned for th pains. In 1882 the new Chief Secreta Lord Frederick Cavendish, and his Und Secretary were assassinated in Phoe Park by the Invincibles, a new terror organisation. As the campaign for Ho Rule gathered momentum, the Gae League, which started the Irish litera renaissance, was established by Doug Hyde and Eóin MacNeill in 18 Conceived as a means of reviving inter in the Irish language and traditional Ir life, the Gaelic League was a responsible for a remarkable litera revival resulting in the formation of t Abbey Theatre in 1904, where plays J M Synge, Sean O'Casey and W B Yea amongst others, were performed.

In 1905 the Sinn Fein movement w formed, in 1909 the Irish Transport a General Workers Union was set up und the leadership of James Connolly, and 1913 there was a massive stri paralysing the city. In 1914 the Ir Volunteers came into being, largely combat the Ulster Volunteers. These lat were raised by Edward Carson in Janua 1913 to defend the right of Ulster

main united with Great Britain. In 1916 e Irish Volunteers seized the Post Office Lower O'Connell Street as their adquarters and the Easter Rising had gun. It was quickly crushed, but so utally that public conscience, clearly palled, overwhelmingly elected Sinn in at the general election of December 18 with de Valera as the new president. hilst the Dublin faction was openly in pport of the guerrilla bands operating ross the country, the Ulster Unionists t up their own provisional government, d the ambushes and assassinations which characterised the Anglo-Irish War, featuring the notorious Black and Tans, began in bloody earnest. The war ended in the truce of July 1921. Despite the ratification of the Irish Free State in January 1922, a large and dissatisfied faction of leaders in the Irish movement took up arms against their former comrades and seized the Four Courts, which they held for two months. The subsequent shelling ordered by the new Dublin Government destroyed much of O'Connell Street but by the 1930s most of the public buildings had been restored.

OURIST INFORMATION OFFICES

ffolk Street   ☎ (01) 605 7700
en all year

n Laoghaire Ferry Terminal
rivals Hall, Dublin Airport
ggott Street Bridge
e Square, Tallaght
ese are walk in offices only. All are
en all year.

Internet
The official tourism site for Dublin
http://www.visitdublin.com

E-mail
information@dublintourism.ie or
reservations@dublintourism.ie
Accommodation reservations
Freephone ☎ 0800 668 668 66

ATHEDRALS AND CHURCHES

ugustinian Church Thomas Street.
signed by E W Pugin and G C Ashlin in
62 it has a mountainous exterior with
ty side aisles to the nave and 160 foot
gh tower crowned by a spire.
arist Church Cathedral
ristchurch Place.
e Cathedral was founded by
rongbow in 1173 on the site of a church
unded in 1038 by Dunan, Bishop of
blin. It is, along with St. Patrick's, one
the best examples in Ireland of early
thic architecture and was extensively
stored between 1871–78 by George
mund Street.
anciscan Church Merchant's Quay.
signed by Patrick Byrne in 1830.
Anne's Church Dawson Street.
signed by Isaac Wells in 1720 with a
manesque-style facade added by Sir
omas Deane in 1868.
Audoen's Church High Street.
blin's only surviving medieval church,
h a portal of 1190. The bell tower,
stored in the 19thC, has three 15thC bells.
Audoen's RC Church High Street.
signed by Patrick Byrne in 1841–47, it
s a monumental, cliff-like exterior with

a huge Corinthian portico added by
Stephen Ashlin in 1898.
St George's Temple Street.
This neo-classical church was designed by
Francis Johnston in 1802 and has a 200
foot high steeple modelled on St Martin-
in-the Fields, London.
St Mary's Mary Street.
A handsome galleried church designed
by Thomas Burgh in 1627.
St Mary's Abbey Meetinghouse Lane.
A Cistercian foundation, established in
1139, whose remains include a fine
vaulted Chapter House of 1190.
St Mary's Pro-Cathedral
Cathedral Street.
A Greek Doric style building, built
1815–25 by John Sweetman and
modelled on the Church of St Philippe,
rue St Honore, Paris.
St Michan's Church Church Street.
Founded in 1095 and largely rebuilt in
1685. Famous for the mummified bodies
in the crypt and its fine 18thC organ.
St Patrick's Cathedral Patrick Street.
The National Cathedral of the Church of
Ireland, it was built between 1220–54 and
was restored in the 19thC.

St Saviour's Dominick Street.
Designed by J J McCarthy in 1858 this extravagant French style Gothic edifice has a bold west door under a triangular hood, crowned by a large rose window.

St Stephen's Mount Street Crescent.
Designed by John Bowden in 1824 this handsome neo-classical church has a Erechtheon inspired Greek style portico.

St Werburgh's Church
Werburgh Street.
Originally the site of an Anglo-Norma foundation, the present church was bu in 1715–19 and rebuilt in 1759–6 following a fire.

Whitefriar Street Carmelite Chur
Stands on the site of a pre-Reformatio Carmelite Priory.

PLACES OF INTEREST

Arbour Hill Collins Barracks.
Cemetery where the leaders of the Easter Rising are buried.

Ashtown Castle Visitor Centre
Pheonix Park.
The oldest building in the park has now been renovated and houses a visitor centre.

Bank of Ireland College Green.
Designed by Sir Edward Lovett Pearce in 1729. It was originally the Parliament House; the first of a series of great public buildings erected in 18thC Dublin.

Bank of Ireland Arts Centre
Foster Place
Contains the Story of Banking Museum, which reflects the role played by the Bank of Ireland in the economic and social development of Ireland.

City Hall Lord Edward Street.
Completed in 1779, this fine building was designed as The Royal Exchange. It features a beautiful coffered dome.

Custom House Custom House Quay.
This masterpiece was designed by James Gandon in 1781 and has a magnificent long river frontage, A Visitor Centre includes a James Gandon Museum and a history of the Custom House itself

Drimnagh Castle Long Mile Road.
Ireland's only castle with a flooded moat. This 13thC castle now has a fully restored Great Hall and 17thC style garden which is open to the public.

Dublin Castle Cork Hill, Dame Street.
The Castle was originally built 1204–28 as part of Dublin's defensive system. The Record or Wardrobe Tower is the principal remnant of the 13thC Anglo-Norman fortress and has walls 16 feet thick.

The 15thC Bermingham Tower was once the state prison where Red Hugh O'Donnell was interned in the 16thC. Of interest are the State Apartments, dating from the British Administration; these were once the residence of Engli Viceroys.

The State Apartments, Undercroft a Chapel Royal are open to the public.

Dublin Civic Museum South Willia Street. ☎ 6794260.
Permanent exhibition about the city Dublin.

Dublin Experience, The Trinity Colleg
An audiovisual presentation of the sto of Dublin.

Dublin's Viking Adventure
Essex Street West
A reconstruction of the sights, soun and smells of life in Viking Dublin, alo with an exhibition of Viking artefac discovered in the area.

Dublin Writers Museum Parnell Squa North. ☎ 8722077.
Traces the history of Irish literature fro its earliest times to the 20thC.

Dublinia Christ Church ☎ 6794611
A realistic sight-and-sound recreation Dublin in medieval times.

Dunsink Observatory between Fingl and Blanchardstown.
Founded in 1783, it is one of the olde observatories in the world. Public nigh are held on the first and third Wednesda of each month from September to Mar inclusive at 8pm–10pm.

Four Courts Inns Quay.
Originally designed by James Gandon 1785, it was destroyed by a fire in 19 but later rebuilt. Four Courts has a 4 foot river frontage and a square cent block with circular hall, crowned by shallow dome carried in a high column drum.

GAA Museum Croke Park. ☎ 855817 The Gaelic Athletic Association (GAA) Ireland's largest sporting and cultu organisation. The museum is in Cro Park, the home of Irish hurling a football, and traces the history of t game and its place in Irish culture.

rden of Remembrance Parnell
uare.
e Garden of Remembrance, opened in
6, dedicated to all those who died in
cause of Irish Freedom.
neral Post Office O'Connell Street.
signed by Francis Johnston and
npleted in 1818. The 1916 Easter
ing started here.
inness Brewery Crane Street.
ablished in 1759 and is now the largest
orting brewery in the world. The
inness Hop Store is open to the public
n – Sat 9.30 am to 4 pm. Sun 12.00 to
n. ☎ 4084800.
inness Hop Store Crane Street.
4084800. Mon-Sat 9.30am–4.00pm
n 12.00–4.00 pm. Documentary films
d exhibition about the company's
velopment.
'penny Bridge Crampton Quay.
elegant pedestrian bridge spanning
Liffey.
raldic Museum Kildare Street
6777444
strates the uses of heraldry and is the
y one of its kind in the world.
sh Architectural Archive Merrion
uare. ☎ 6763430.
sh-Jewish Museum 3 Walworth
ad. ☎ 4531797
sh Museum of Modern Art Royal
spital, Kilmainham. ☎ 6129900.
mes Joyce Centre North Great
orge's Street ☎ 8788547
nuseum in a Georgian mansion, built
1784, devoted to the great novelist.
mes Joyce Museum Sandycove.
2809265.
sonal possessions, photographs, first
tions and items about James Joyce.
mainham Jail Inchicore Road.
4535984.
It in 1796. Museum dedicated to the
h patriots imprisoned there from 1792-
4, including Emmet and his United
hmen colleagues, the Fenians, the
incibles and the Irish Volunteers of the
ter Rising. It was closed in 1924 and
pened as a museum in 1966.
g's Inns Constitution Hill and
rrietta Street.
lorious classical edifice, partly built to
plans of James Gandon. The courtyard
s Henrietta Street where one can see
blin's earliest Georgian mansions.
inster House Kildare Street.
ginally a handsome town mansion
signed by Richard Castle for the Earl of

Kildare in 1745; it has been the Parliament
House since 1922.
Malahide Castle Malahide.
Originally built in 1185, it was the seat of
the Talbot family from 1185–1976. Now in
public ownership, it displays a large part
of the National Portrait collection and the
Fry Model Railway Museum.
Marino Casino Malahide Road.
A miniature Palladian style masterpiece
designed by Sir William Chambers in
1762. Built as a little pleasure house
beside Lord Charlemont's country
residence for the enormous sum of
£60,000, it's a remarkably compact
building planned in a Greek cross
articulated by both free standing columns
and pilasters with rusticated main walls.
The circular hall inside, ringed by
columns, is crowned by a coffered dome.
The graceful urns crowning the attic
storey are chimneys.
Mansion House Dawson Street.
Built in 1705, it has been the official
residence of the Lord Mayor of Dublin
since 1715.
National Maritime Museum Haigh
Terrace, Dun Laoghaire.
☎ 2800969. (Summer only).
Traces the history of Irish Literature from
its earliest times up to the 20thC.
National Museum Kildare Street.
☎ 6777444
Houses a fabulous collection of national
antiquities including Bronze Age gold
ornaments.
National Museum (Collins Barracks)
Benburb Street ☎ 6777444
Ireland's museum of decorative arts and
it's economic, social, political and military
history, based in the oldest military
barracks in Europe.
National Print Museum Haddington
Road. ☎ 6603770
Situated in the former Garrison Chapel in
Beggars Bush Barracks, the museum
houses a unique collection of implements
and machines from Ireland's printing
industry.
National Transport Museum Howth
Castle Demesne ☎ 8480831
A collection of buses, trams, commercial,
military and fire appliances, along with
other memorabilia from the transport
industry.
National Wax Museum Granby Row.
☎ 8726340.
Wax replicas of well-known persons and
scenes.

Natural History Museum Merrion Street. ☎ 6777444
Houses a collection of preserved animals and the remains of extinct mammals and birds.

Newman House St Stephen's Green.
Built in 1765 for Richard Whaley MP with plasterwork by Robert West, the house has also been owned by the celebrated gambler Buck Whaley.

Number 29 Lower Fitzwilliam Street. ☎ 7026165
This typical four-storey-over-basement street house has been restored and furnished exactly as it would have been during the late 18thC.

Old Jameson Distillery Bow Street.
See the art of Irish Whiskey making through an audiovisual presentation and guided tour of the old distillery.

Pearse Museum St. Edna's Park, Grange Road. ☎ 4934208
Housed in a former school, this museum is dedicated to Patrick Pearse and includes an audiovisual presentation and a nature study room with displays on Irish flora and fauna.

Powerscourt House South William Street. A classical style mansion designed by Robert Mack and built between 1771–74, now a lively centre of shops, cafés and restaurants.

Rathfarnham Castle Rathfarnham.
Dating from around 1583, this castle has 18thC interiors by Sir William Chambers and James Stuart and is presented to visitors as a castle undergoing conservation.

Royal Hospital Kilmainham.
Dublin's only monumental 17thC build was built as a home for army pension and has one of Dublin's finest interiors also houses the Irish Museum of Mod Art.

Shaw Birthplace, The Synge Stree ☎ 4750854
The birthplace of one of Ireland's th Nobel prizewinners for literature.

Temple Bar This charming area Dublin's Bohemian quarter. With narrow cobbled streets running clos the Liffey it is full of character. It is he to artists and musicians of all styles talents.

Trinity College College Green.
The original Elizabethan college founded in 1592 but the present buil was built between 1755–1759. cruciform complex wrapped aro quadrangles and gardens has impressive 300 foot Palladian fac designed by Henry Keene and J Sanderford.
The library's great treasures include 8thC Book of Kells, the Book of Durr the Book of Armagh and the L Hymnorum.

Waterways Visitor Centre Grand C Basin, Ringsend ☎ 6777510.
A centre built on piers over the ca housing an exhibition of Irela waterways.

Wood Quay by Christchurch Cathedr Modern office blocks and new c offices occupy this site which was c the 9th–11thC Viking city of Dublin.

LIBRARIES

Central Library Ilac Centre. ☎ 8734333.
Central Catholic Library Merrion Square. ☎ 6761264.
Religious and general interest, with a large Irish section.

Gilbert Library Pearse Street. ☎ 6777662.
Irish interest books including references to local printing and bookbinding.

Goethe Institut Library Merrion Square. ☎ 6611155.
A business information centre.

Kings Inns Henrietta Street. ☎ 8744840.
Founded 1787, contains over 100,000 books and copies of almost all of the Dublin directories ever published.

Marsh's Library St Patrick's Close. ☎ 4543511.
Opened in 1701, contains many books.

National Library Kildare Street. ☎ 6030200
Offers over half a million books, as as a vast collection of maps, prints manuscripts and an invaluable collec of Irish newspapers.

Royal Irish Academy 19 Dawson Str ☎ 6762570, 6764222.
One of the largest collections of anc Irish manuscripts in the country.

Trinity College Library College Gre ☎ 6082308.

oldest and most famous of Dublin's
aries; it houses over a million books
s a magnificent collection of early
minated manuscripts, including the
ous Book of Kells.

Other general and reference libraries:
Dublin Diocesan Library Clonliffe
Road. ☎ 8741680.
Genealogical Office Kildare Street.
☎ 6030200.

LLERIES, ARTS CENTRES, CONCERT AND EXHIBITION HALLS

nk of Ireland Arts Centre
ter Place. ☎ 6711488
y Arts Centre Moss Street.
5770643
ew complex of galleries, exhibition
as and theatre space for local groups
d artists.
uglas Hyde Gallery Trinity College.
5081116.
llery of Photography Meeting
use Square. ☎ 6714654.
**gh Lane Municipal Gallery of
dern Art** Parnell Square North.
3741903.
tional Concert Hall Earlsfort Terrace.
4751572.

National Gallery Merrion Square West.
☎ 6615133.
Point, The North Wall Quay. ☎ 8363633
Project Arts Centre East Essex.
☎ 6712321.
RHA Gallagher Gallery Ely Place.
☎ 6612558
Royal Dublin Society Ballsbridge.
☎ 6680866.
Solomon Gallery Powerscourt Centre.
☎ 6794237.
Taylor Galleries Kildare St. ☎ 6766055.
United Arts Club Fitzwilliam Street
Upper. ☎ 6762965.

RKS AND GARDENS

agh Gardens Clonmel Street
signed by Ninian Niven in 1863, this is
e of the least known and most tranquil
Dublin's parks.
rley Park
uated in Rathfarnham this large park
tains areas of woodland, a large pond,
ure trail and model railway.
tional Botanic Gardens
ated in Glasnevin, it provides 50 acres
magnificent gardens with a fabulous
lection of plants, shrubs and trees;
ablished in 1790. Many of the plants
ne from tropical Africa and South
erica.
oenix Park
oenix Park, covering over 1,760 acres,
the best-known park in Ireland.
closed by an 8 mile long stone wall, the
k was laid out in the mid 18thC and
s the scene of the Phoenix Park
rders in 1882, when the Chief
cretary and Under-Secretary for Ireland
re assassinated. The park includes a
mber of buildings, the most important
which is Aras an Uachtarain; a private
use built in 1751, it later became the
use of the President of Ireland when Dr
uglas Hyde moved there in 1938.

Other buildings are the houses of the
Pope's ambassador and the American
ambassador; St Mary's Hospital with
handsome chapel by Thomas Cooley of
1771; the Magazine Fort of 1734. There is
the people's gardens by the main
entrance on Parkgate Street, and a zoo.
St Anne's Park
St Anne's Park, to the north east in
Dollymount, is a large park covering over
270 acres and wooded with evergreen,
oak, pine, beech, chestnut and lime.
There is a lovely rose garden, opened in
1975. Formerly the house of the
Guinness Family.
St Stephen's Green
In the heart of the city, St Stephen's Green
was originally an open common, enclosed
in 1663. The earliest as well as the largest
of Dublin's squares, it is encircled by
magnificent 18thC and 19thC buildings, in
particular No 85, by Richard Castle in
1739; No 86 by Robert West in 1765; on
the west side, Nos 119-20 by Richard
Castle and the Royal College of Surgeons
by Edward Pike in 1806. The Green itself
was opened to the general public in 1877.
War Memorial Gardens Islandbridge.
Dedicated to the memory of the Irish

soldiers who died in World War 1, these pleasant gardens include a sunken rose garden and herbaceous borders.

Zoological Gardens
The Zoological Gardens, inside Phoenix Park, are famous for the breeding of li and other 'big cats'. The zoo attractive gardens encircling two nat lakes where pelicans, flamingoes, du and geese abound.

ENTERTAINMENT, FOOD AND DRINK
CABARET

Abbey Tavern Howth. ☎ 8390282.
Burlington Hotel Leeson Street Upper. ☎ 6605222.

Clontarf Castle Clontarf. ☎ 8332321.
Jury's Hotel Ballsbridge. ☎ 6605000.

RESTAURANTS

Adrian's Howth ☎ 8391696
Ante Room Baggot Street Lower. ☎ 6625098
Ayumi-Ya Restaurant Blackrock. ☎ 2831767
Chapter One Parnell Square. ☎ 8732266
China-Sichuan Restaurant Stillorgan. ☎ 2880375
Commons Restaurant St. Stephen's Green. ☎ 4780530
Cooke's Cafe South William Street. ☎ 6790536
Ernie's Restaurant Donnybrook. ☎ 2693300
Fitzers Ballsbridge. ☎ 6671301
Les Freres Jacques Dame Street. ☎ 6794555
Grey Door,The Pembroke Street Upper. ☎ 6763286.
King Sitric Howth. ☎ 8325235.
Le Coq Hardi Ballsbridge. ☎ 6689070.
Lord Edward Christchurch Place. ☎ 4542420.

Old Dublin Francis Street. ☎ 4542028
Pasta Fresca Chatham Street. ☎ 6684563
Peacock Alley South William Street. ☎ 6620760
QV2 St. Andrew Street. ☎ 6773363
Restaurant Na Mara Dun Laoghaire. ☎ 2806767.
Restaurant Patrick Guilbaud Upper Merrion Street. ☎ 6764192
Rolys Bistro, Ballsbridge Terrace. ☎ 6682611
Shalimar South Great Georges Street. ☎ 6710738
La Stampa Dawson Street. ☎ 677861
Tosca Suffolk Street. ☎ 6796744
Tracadero St. Andrew Street. ☎ 6775545
Wrights Fishermans Wharf, Custom House Docks. ☎ 6701900
Yamamori Noodles South Great Georges Street. ☎ 4755001

PUBS AND BARS

Abbey Tavern (trad music) Howth. ☎ 8390307.
Auld Dubliner Anglesea Street, Temple Bar. ☎ 6770527
Baggot Inn Lower Baggot Street. ☎ 6761430
Bleeding Horse Upper Camden Street. ☎ 4752705
Brazen Head Bridge Street Lower. ☎ 6779549
Cafe en Seine Dawson Street. ☎ 6774369
The Chocolate Bar Upper Hatch Street. ☎ 4780166

Davy Byrnes Duke Street. ☎ 6775217
Doheny and Nesbitt Lower Baggot Street. ☎ 6762945.
Horseshoe Bar, Shelbourne Hotel St. Stephen's Green. ☎ 6766471
Houricans Leeson Street. ☎ 6762634.
Hughes Bar Chancery Street. ☎ 872654
International Bar Wicklow Street. ☎ 6779250
Kehoe's South Anne Street. ☎ 677831
Kitty O'Shea's Grand Canal Street. ☎ 6609965.
Long Hall Great George Street. ☎ 4751590.

McDaids Harry Street. ☎ 6794395.
Mulligans Poolbeg Street. ☎ 6775582.
The Norseman East Essex Street,
Temple Bar. ☎ 6715135
O'Donoghues (trad music) Merrion
Row. ☎ 6607194
O'Sheas Merchant Lower Bridge
Street. ☎ 6796793
Oliver St. John Gogarty Fleet Street.
☎ 6711822

Palace Bar Fleet Street. ☎ 6779290.
Porterhouse Brewing Company
Parliament Street. ☎ 6798847
Ryans Parkgate Street. ☎ 6776097.
Slattery's (trad music) Rathmines Road.
☎ 4972052.
Stag's Head Dame Court. ☎ 6793701.
The Temple Bar Temple Bar. ☎ 6773807
Toners Lower Baggot Street. ☎ 6763090
Whelans Wexford Street. ☎ 4752649

NIGHTCLUBS

Annabelle's, Burlington Hotel Upper
Lesson Street. ☎ 6605222
Kitchen, Clarence Hotel East Essex
Street. ☎ 6623066

Mean Fidler Wexford Street. ☎ 4758555
PoD Harcourt Street. ☎ 4780225
Ri Ra Dame Court ☎ 6774835
Temple of Sound Ormond Quay.

THEATRES

Abbey Theatre Abbey Street Lower 1.
☎ 8787222.
Andrews Lane Theatre ☎ 6795720.
Focus Theatre Pembroke Place,
Pembroke Street 2. ☎ 6763071.
Gaiety Theatre South King Street 2.
☎ 6771717.
Gate Theatre Cavendish Row, Parnell
Square. ☎ 8744045.
Lambert Puppet Theatre Clifton Lane,
Monkstown. ☎ 2800974.

Olympia Theatre 74 Dame Street 2.
☎ 6777744.
Peacock Theatre Abbey Street Lower 1.
☎ 8787222.
Project Arts Centre 39 East Essex
Street. ☎ 6712321.
(Temporarily at Henry Place while
premises being rebuilt)
Samuel Beckett Centre Trinity
College. ☎ 6082266
Tivoli Theatre Francis Street. ☎ 4544472

CINEMAS

Ambassador Parnell Street. ☎ 8727000
Classic Cinema Harold's Cross Road 6.
☎ 4923324
Forum Cinema Dun Laoghaire.
☎ 2809574.
Irish Film Centre Eustace Street.
☎ 6778788
Lighthouse Cinema Middle Abbey
Street. ☎ 8730438.
Omniplex 10 Screen Santry.
☎ 8428844

Ormonde Cinema Stillorgan Plaza,
Stillorgan. ☎ 2780000.
Savoy Cinema 19 O'Connell Street
Upper 1. ☎ 8746000.
Screen at D'Olier Street ☎ 6714988
Stella Picture Theatre Ltd 207
Rathmines Road Lower 6. ☎ 4971281.
UCI Blanchardstown ☎ 1850 525354
UCI Coolock ☎ 8485133.
UCI Tallaght ☎ 4522611.
Virgin Cinemas Parnell Street ☎ 8728444

RAIL & BUS TRAVEL

Dublin is linked with the cities and towns
of Ireland by a network of rail and bus
services operated by Coras Iompair
Eireann (CIE), which is Ireland's National
Internal Transport Authority.

All information regarding rail and road
services can be obtained from: CIE, 59
O'Connell Street Upper, Dublin 1.
☎ 8720000.

HOTELS

Ashling Parkgate Street. ☎ 6772324.
Avalon House (Budget Accommodation Centre) Aungier Street. ☎ 4750001.
Berkeley Court Lansdowne Road. ☎ 6601711.
Brooks Drury Street. ☎ 6704000.
Burlington Upper Leeson Street. ☎ 6605222.
Buswells Molesworth Street. ☎ 6764013.
Conrad International Earlsfort Terrace. ☎ 6765555.
Fitzpatrick Castle Killiney. ☎ 2840700.
Forte Posthouse Dublin Airport. ☎ 8444211.
Forte Travelodge Castleknock. ☎ 1800 709709
Forte Travelodge Swords. ☎ 1800 709709.
Great Southern Dublin Airport. ☎ 8446000.
Gresham O'Connell Street Upper. ☎ 8746881.

Holiday Inn Pearse Street. ☎ 6703666.
Jury's Ballsbridge. ☎ 6605000.
Jury's Christchurch. ☎ 4540000
Kildare Hotel & Country Club Straffan. ☎ 6017200.
Morrison Ormond Quay. ☎ 8782999.
Mount Herbert Herbert Road. ☎ 6684321.
Plaza Hotel Tallaght. ☎ 1850 566566.
Royal Dublin O'Connell Street. ☎ 8733666.
Royal Marine Hotel Dun Laoghaire. ☎ 2801911.
Shelbourne Meridian St Stephen's Green. ☎ 6766471.
Doyle Skylon Upper Drumcondra Roa ☎ 8379121.
Doyle Tara Merrion Road. ☎ 2694666.
The Towers Lansdowne Road. ☎ 6670033.
Westbury Grafton Street. ☎ 6791122.

SHOPPING

Arnott's Henry Street. ☎ 8050400.
Brown Thomas Grafton Street. ☎ 6056666.
Clery and Co O'Connell Street Lower. ☎ 8786000.
Georges Arcade Clarendon Street.
Ilac Centre Henry Street.
Jervis Shoppping Centre Mary Street.

Marks & Spencers Grafton Street. ☎ 6797855.
Penney's Stores Mary Street. ☎ 872778
Powerscourt Townhouse Centre Clarendon Street.
Roches Stores Henry Street. ☎ 873004
Royal Hibernian Way Grafton Street.
St. Stephen's Green Shopping Centr

MARKETS

Iveagh Market (old clothes, furniture etc.) Francis Street.
Liberty Market (clothes, fabrics, household goods) Meath Street.
Moore Street Market (fruit and vegetables) off Henry Street.

Mother Redcaps Fri–Sun only Christchurch Back Lane. ☎ 4538306
Temple Bar Square (Food) Saturday only.
Vegetable Market (fruit, vegetables, fish and flowers) St Mitchan's Street.

SPORTS AND ENTERTAINMENT

International Sports Venues
Athletics – *Croke Park GAA* – ☎8363222.
Football – *Lansdowne Road* – ☎6689300.
Rugby – *Lansdowne Road* – ☎ 6689300.

Gaelic Football and Hurling
Croke Park GAA. ☎ 8363222

Golf 18-hole golf clubs:
Beaverstown Golf Club – 10 miles from Dublin.
Beech Park – 10 miles from Dublin.
Blanchardstown Golf Centre – 8 miles from Dublin.
Castle Golf Club – Rathfarnham, 4 miles

...om Dublin.
...astlewarden Golf Club – 12 miles from ...blin
...ontarf Golf Club – 2½ miles from Dublin.
...orballis – Donabate – 13 miles from ...ublin.
...eerpark Hotel and Golf Courses – Howth 9 miles from Dublin.
...onabate – 13 miles from Dublin.
...un Laoghaire – 7 miles from Dublin.
...dmondstown – 6 miles from Dublin.
...m Park – 3½ miles from Dublin.
...orrest Little Golf Club – 5½ miles from ...ublin.
...range Rathfarnham – 6 miles from Dublin.
...ermitage Lucan – 7¼ miles from Dublin.
...owth – 9 miles from Dublin.
...land Malahide – 9 miles from Dublin.
...ucan – 8 miles from Dublin.
...uttrelstown Golf & Country Club – 6 miles ...om Dublin
...illtown – 4½ miles from Dublin.
...ewlands Clondalkin – 6 miles from Dublin.
...pen Golf Centre – 6 miles from Dublin.
...ortmarnock – 9 miles from Dublin.
...oyal Dublin – Dollymount, 3 miles from ...ublin.

St. Margarets Golf Club – 8 miles from Dublin.
Slade Valley – Saggart, 9 miles from Dublin.
Stackstown – 9 miles from Dublin.
Swords – 10 miles from Dublin.
Westmanstown – 6 miles from Dublin.
Woodbrook – near Bray, 11½ miles from Dublin.

Greyhound Racing

Greyhound racing is one of Ireland's leading spectator sports. Meetings are held at:
Shelbourne Park Stadium – Ringsend (Wed, Thurs and Sat at 8pm).
Harold's Cross Stadium – (Mon, Tues, and Fri at 8 pm).

Horse Racing

There are two racecourses on the outskirts of Dublin:
Leopardstown – 6 miles from Dublin.
Fairyhouse – 12 miles from Dublin.

Leisure Centre (various sports)
Ballyfermot

HOSPITALS

eaumont Beaumont Road. ☎ 8377755.
lackrock Clinic Rock Road. ☎ 2832222.
ames Connolly Blanchardstown. ☎ 8213844.
later Misericordiae Eccles Street. ☎ 8301122.
later Private Eccles Street. ☎8384444.
otunda Hospital Parnell Square. ☎ 8730700

St. Brendan's Grangegorman Upper ☎ 8385844
St. James James Street. ☎ 4537941.
St. Michaels Lower George Street, Dun Laoghaire. ☎ 2806901.
St. Michaels (Pte) Crofton Road, Dun Laoghaire. ☎ 2808411.
St. Patrick's James's St. ☎ 6775423.
St. Vincents Elm Park. ☎ 2694533.

GARDA SIOCHANA (POLICE)

Greater Dublin Area Headquarters ...hoenix Park. ☎ 6771156.

Dublin Metropolitan Area Headquarters Harcourt Square. ☎ 4755555.

EMBASSIES

American ☎ 6688777
Apostolic Nunciature ☎ 8380577
Arab Republic of Egypt ☎ 6606566
Australian ☎ 6761517
British ☎ 2053700
Canadian ☎ 4781988
French ☎ 2601666
German ☎ 2693011

Italian ☎ 6601744
Japanese ☎ 2694244
Netherlands ☎ 2693444
Norwegian ☎ 6621800
Spanish ☎ 2691640
Swedish ☎ 6715822
Swiss ☎ 2692515

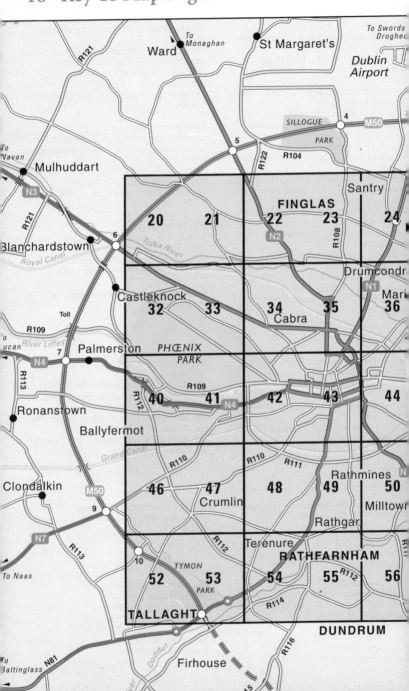

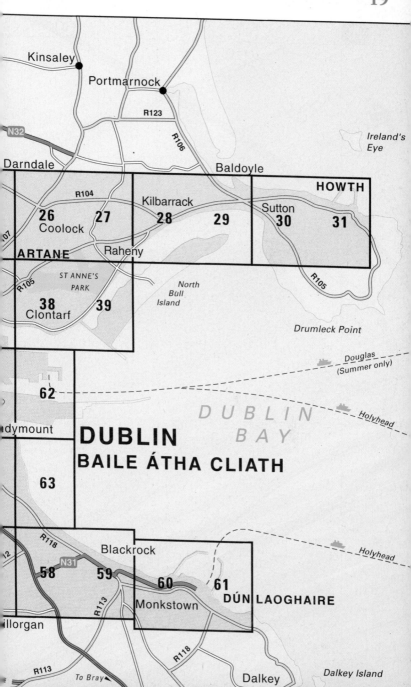

Kinsaley

Portmarnock

R123

R106

N32

Darndale

Baldoyle

Ireland's Eye

HOWTH

R104

Kilbarrack

26
Coolock
27

28
29

Sutton
30

31

ARTANE

Raheny

R105

St ANNE'S PARK

North Bull Island

38
Clontarf
39

Drumleck Point

62

Douglas (Summer only)

Holyhead

dymount

DUBLIN
BAILE ÁTHA CLIATH

DUBLIN BAY

63

R118

Blackrock

Holyhead

N31

58

59

60

61

DÚN LAOGHAIRE

R113

Monkstown

illorgan

R118

R113

To Bray

Dalkey

Dalkey Island

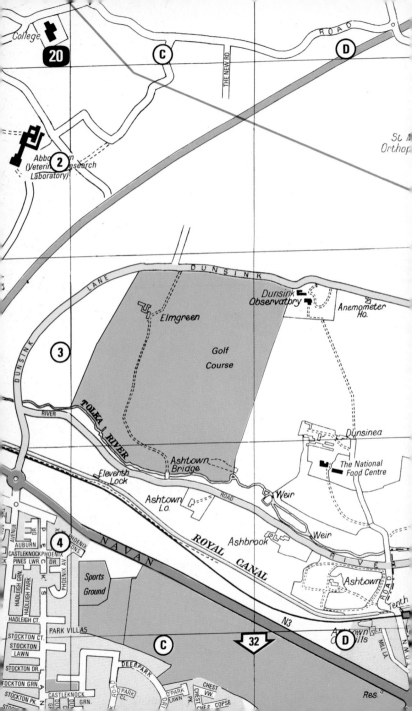

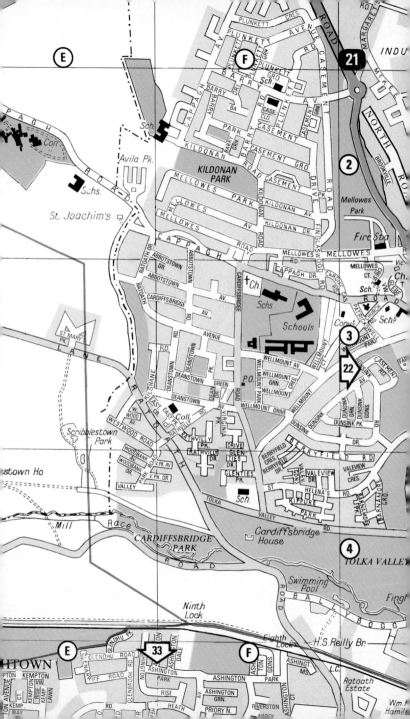

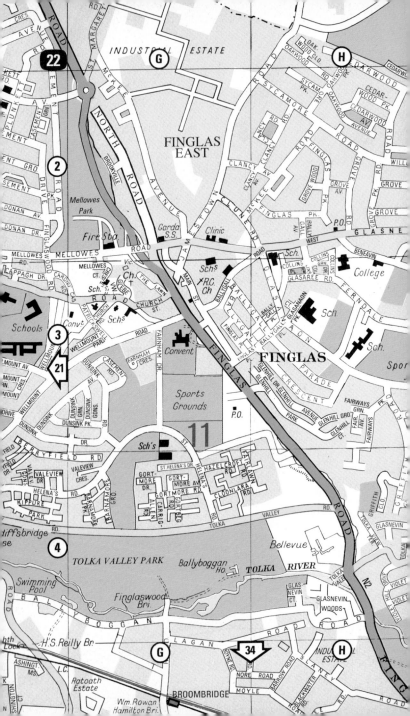

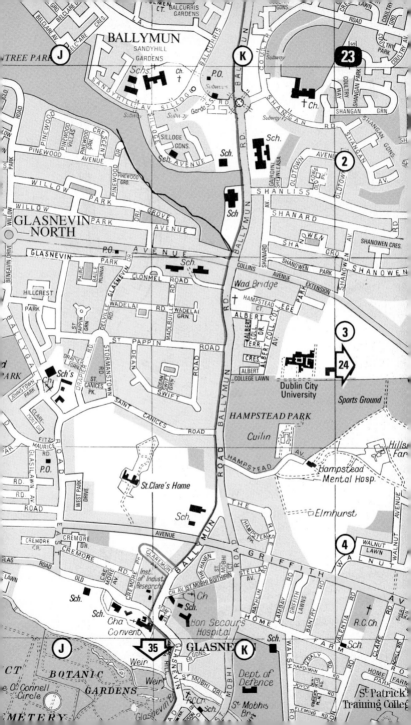

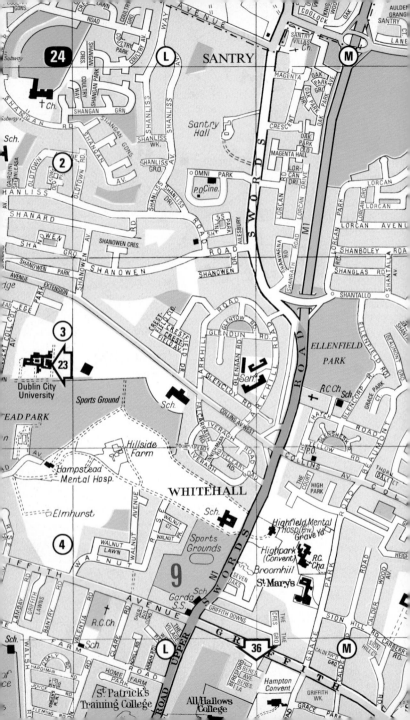

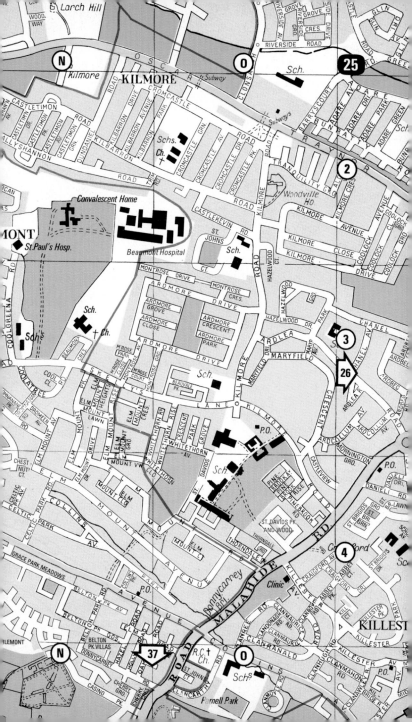

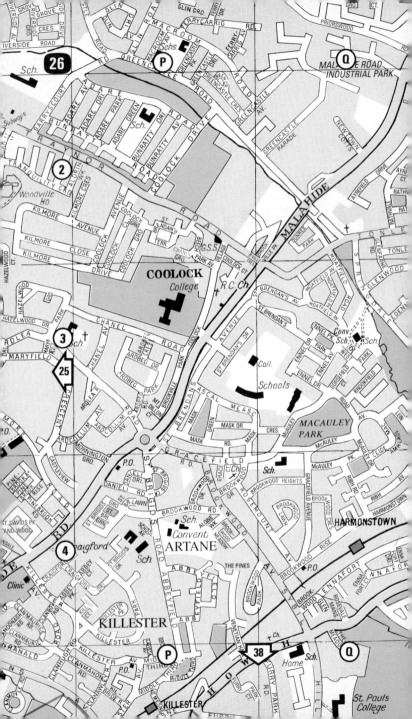

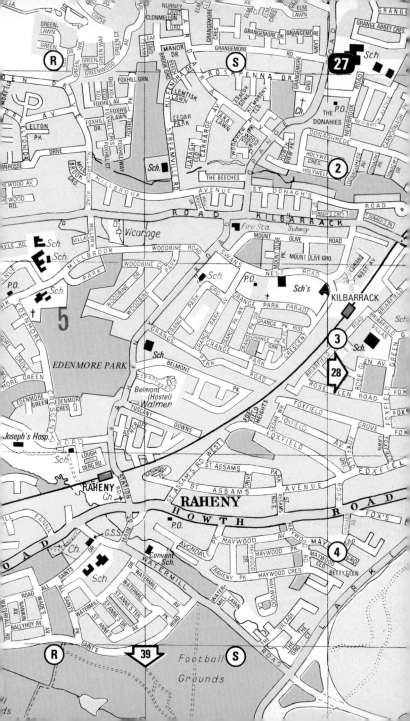

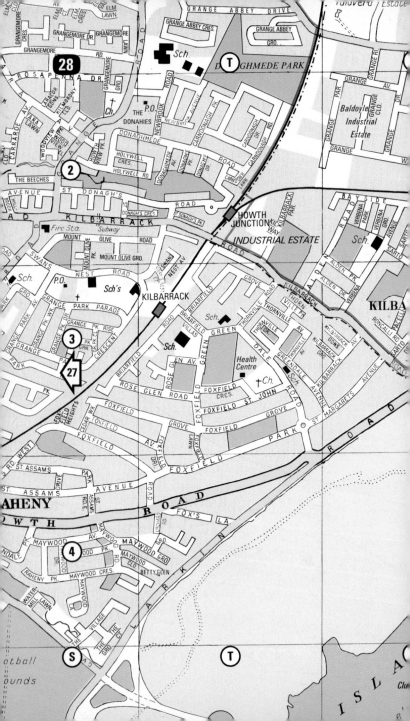

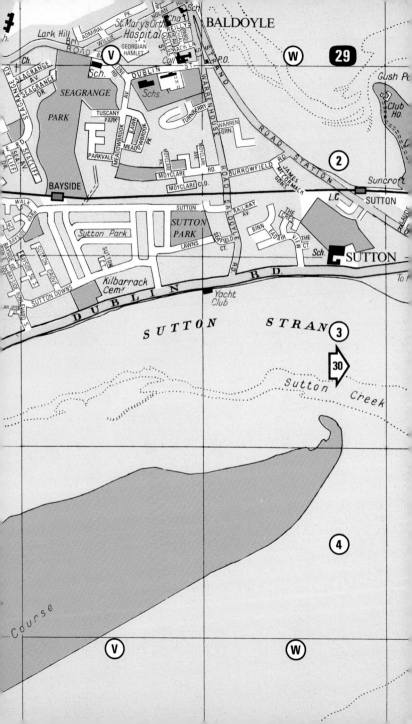

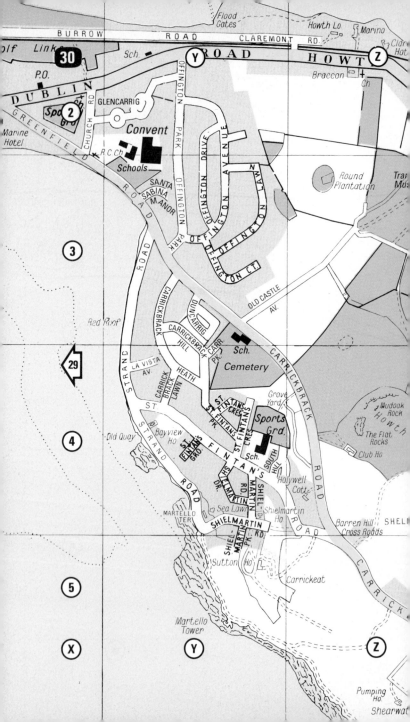

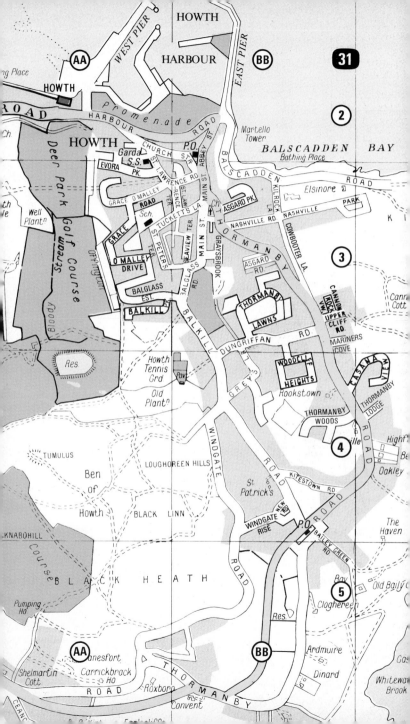

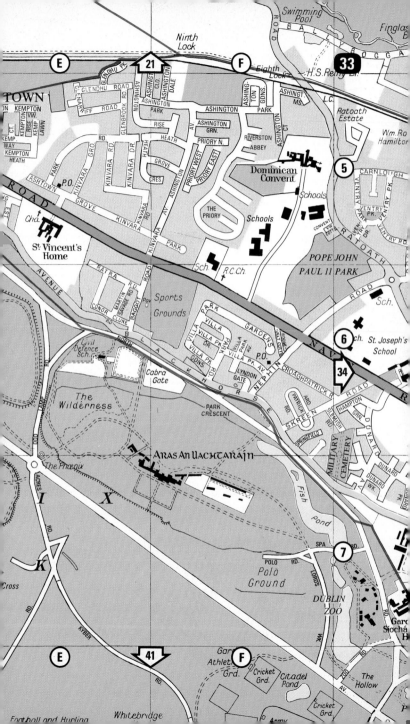

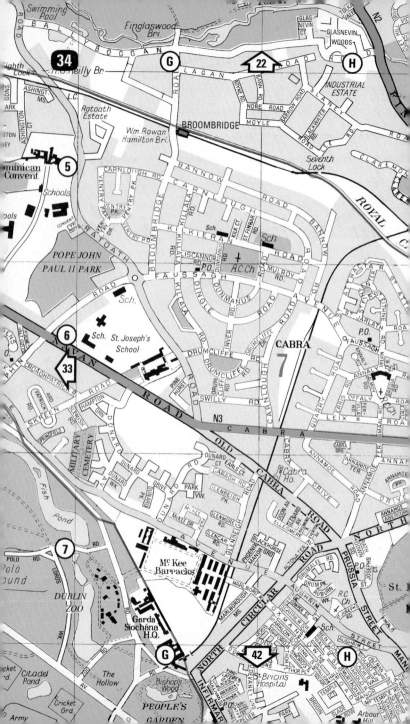

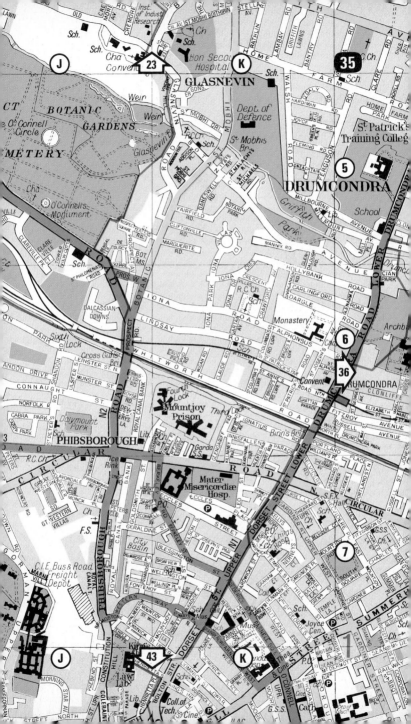

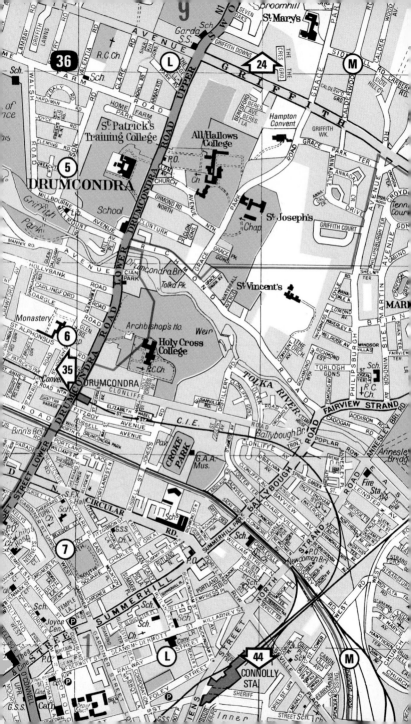

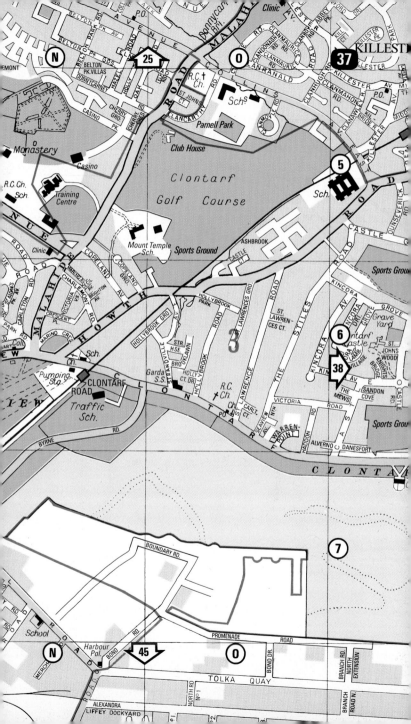

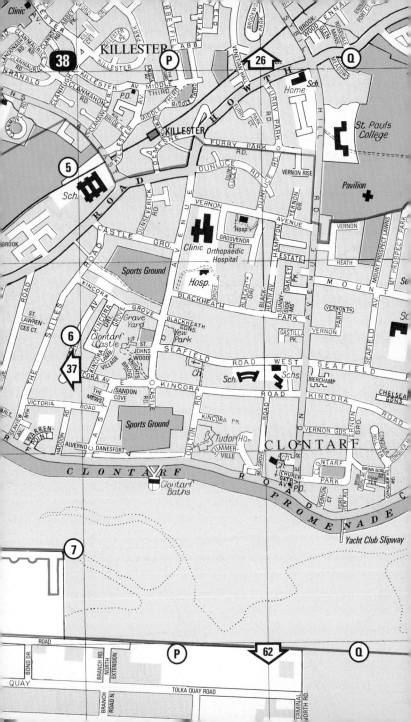

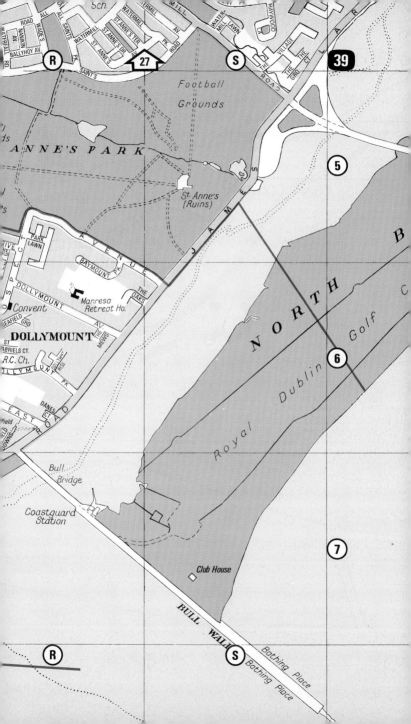

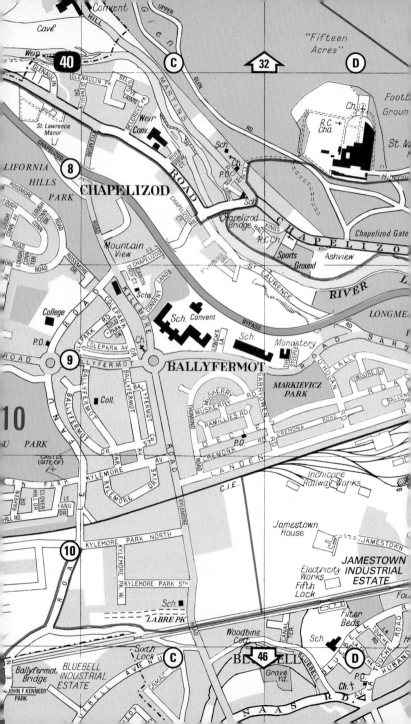

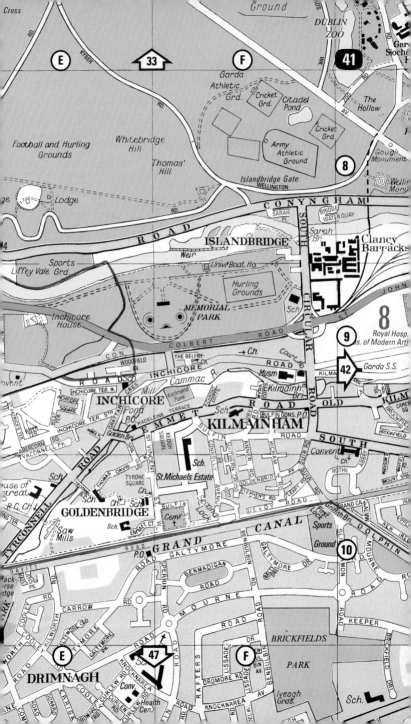

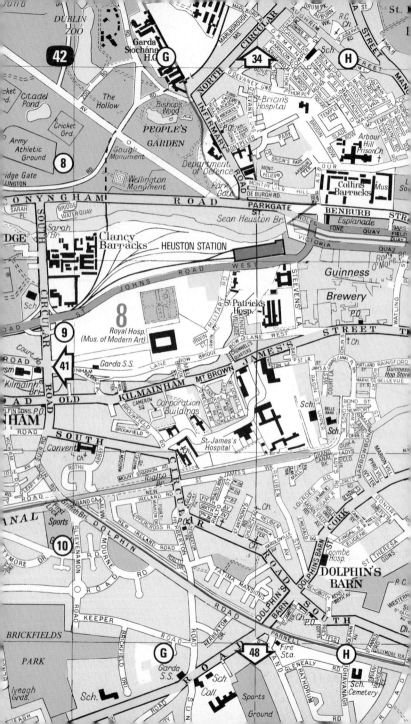

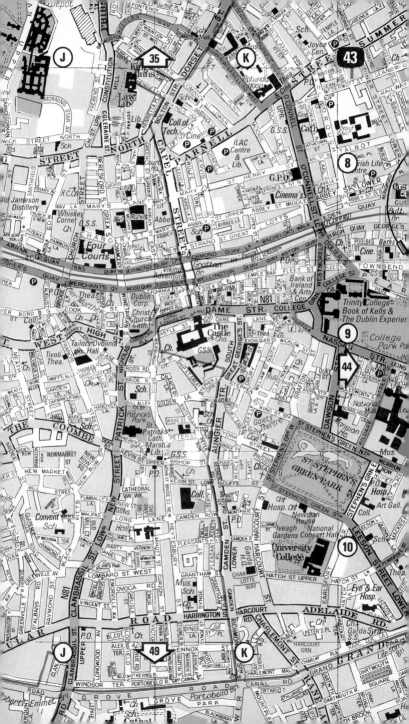

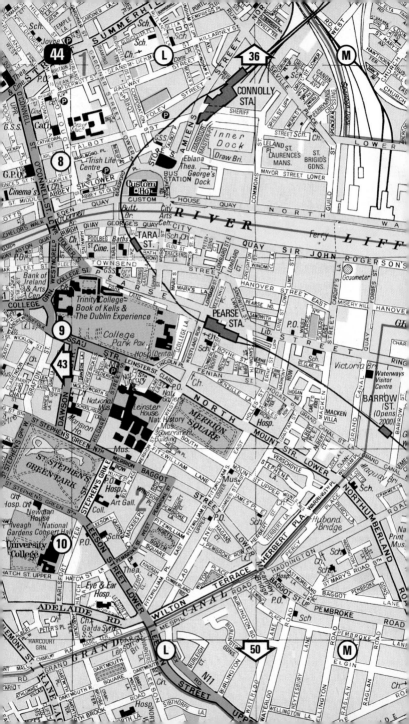

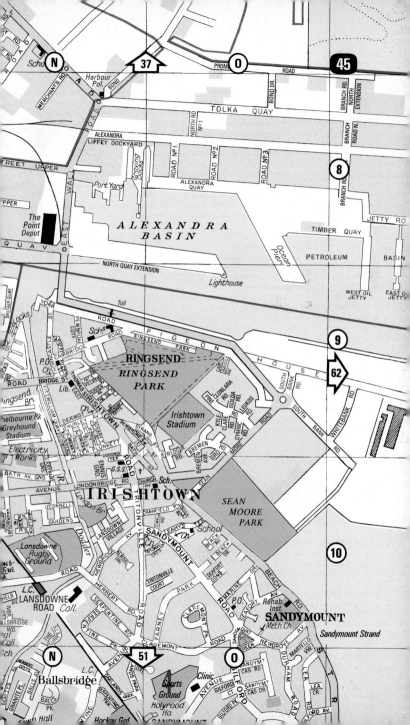

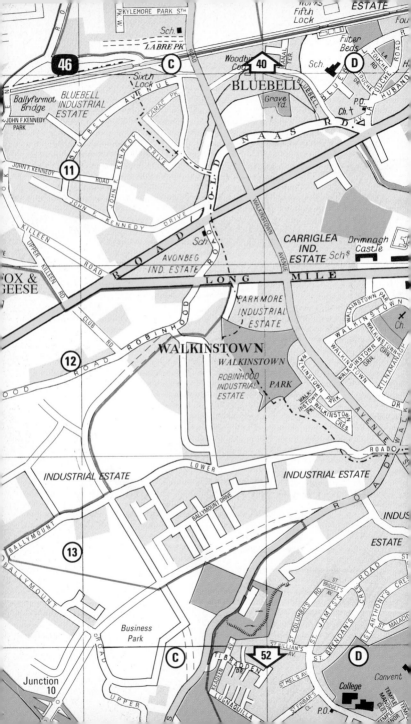

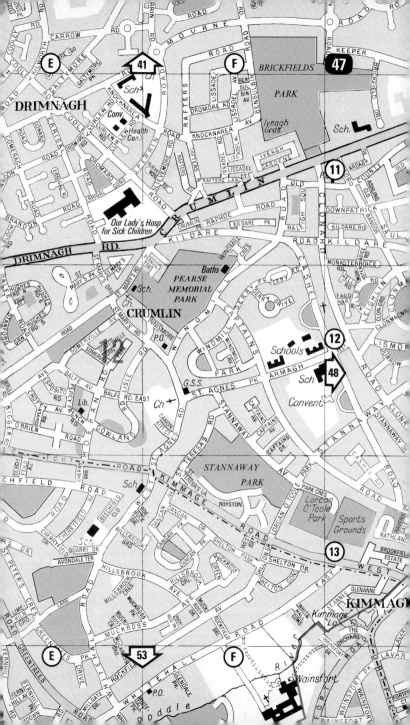

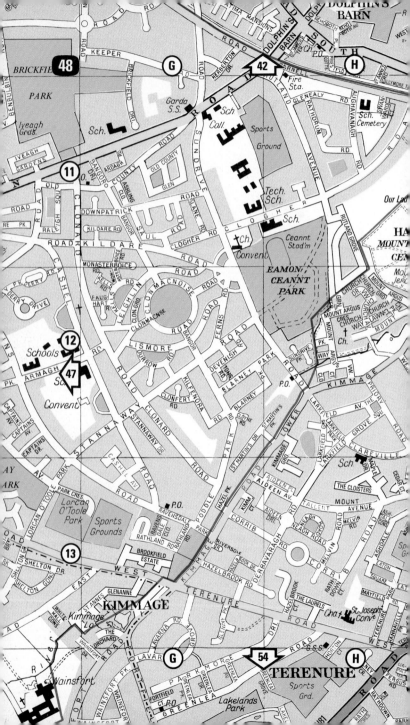

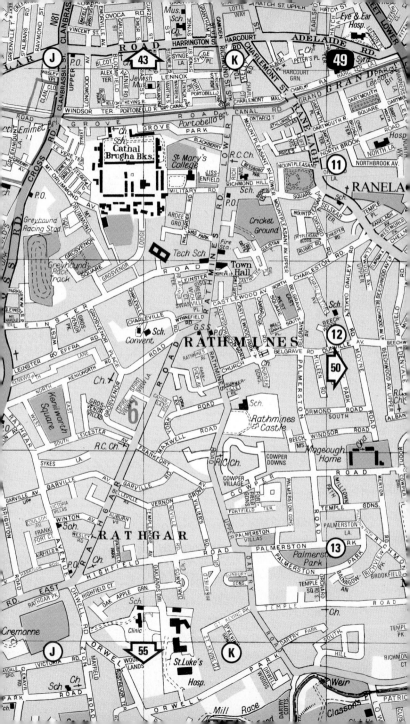

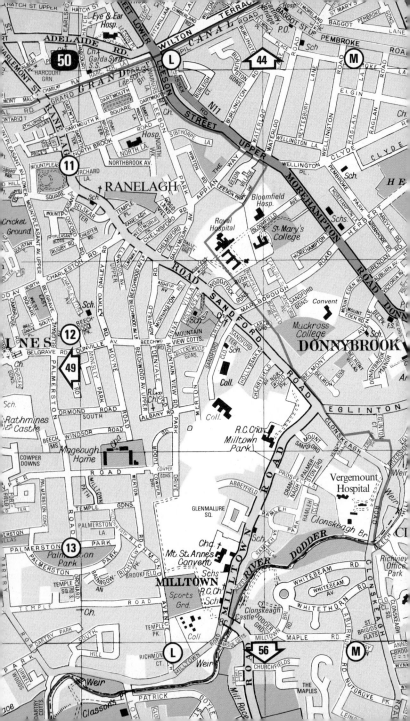

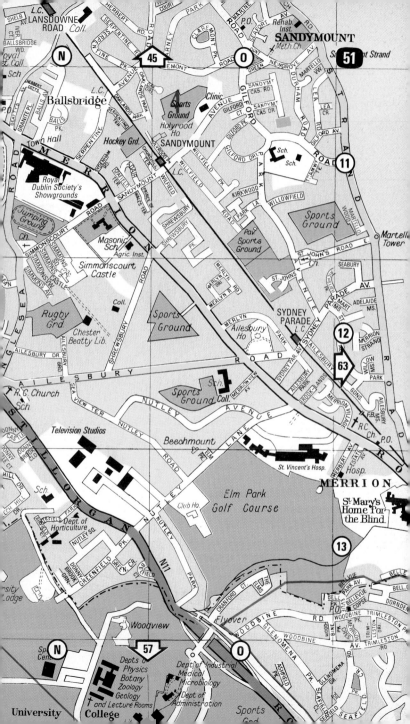

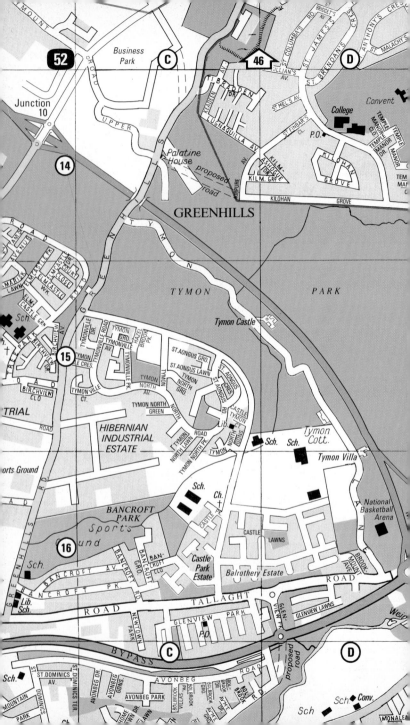

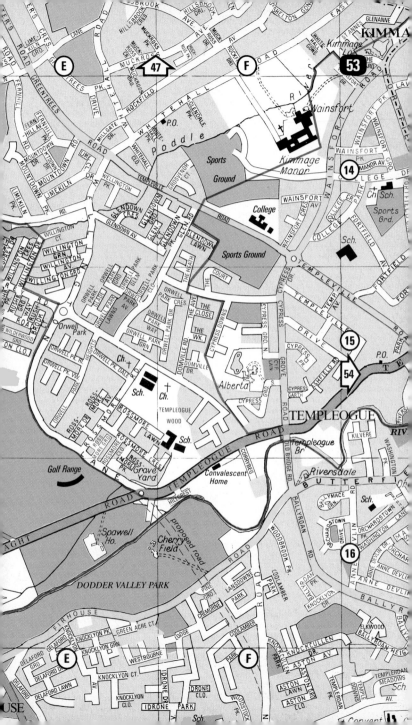

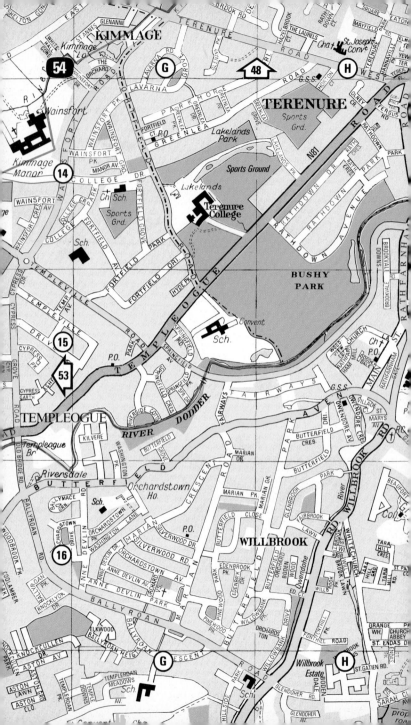

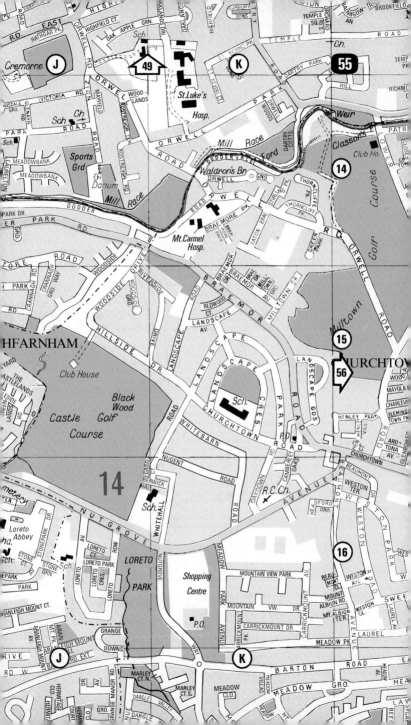

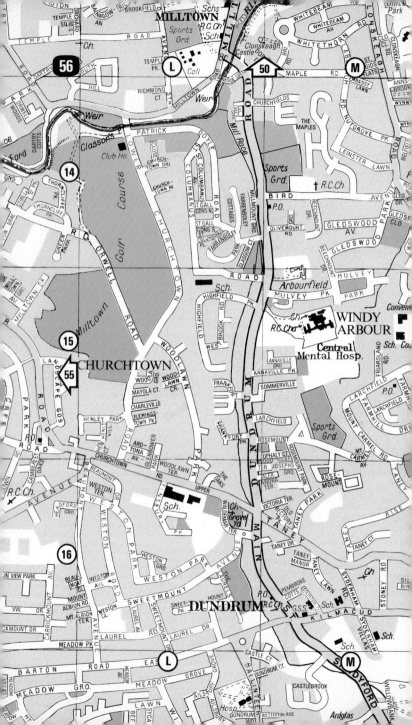

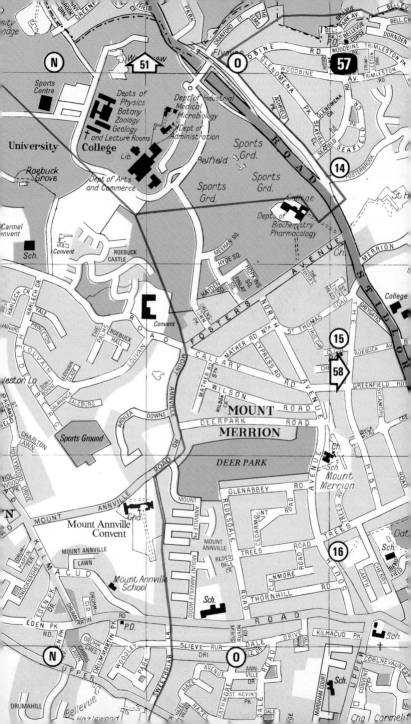

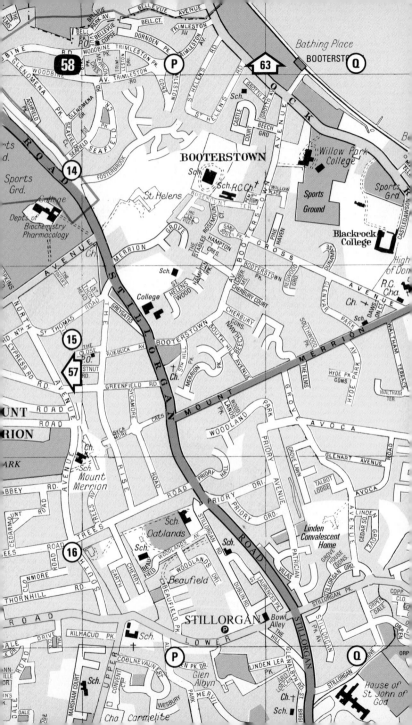

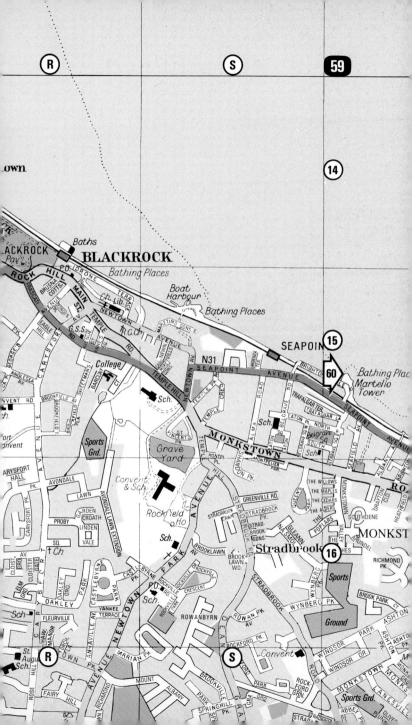

R   S   **59**

14

Baths
BLACKROCK
ACKROCK
Pav.
Bathing Places
ROCK HILL
Boat
Harbour
Bathing Places
NEWTOWN
College
SEAPOINT   **15**
N31
SEAPOINT   AVENUE
60
Bathing Plac.
Martello
Tower
Sch.
Sch.
St. VINCENT'S PK
MONKSTOWN
Sch.
Sports
Grd.
Grave
Yard
Convent
& Sch.
Rockfield
Ho.
GREENVILLE RD.
Stradbrook
THE WILLOWS
THE MAPLES
THE CEDARS
THE ALDERS
MONKST
ARYSFORT
HALL
AVONDALE
Sch.
Stradbrook
THE
POPLARS
SOUTHDENE
RICHMOND
PK
MONKST
Brooklawn
Stradbrook
16
Sports
Ground
PROBY
GARDEN
CROATH
LINDEN
VALE
Ch
SQ.
BROOK
LAWN
WD.
STRADBROOK
WYNBERG
BROOK PARK PK.
YANKEE
TERRACE
Sch.
ROWANBYRN
ROWAN PK.
St. Aug.
Sch.   **R**   FLEURVILLE
MARIAN PK.
Rockford PK.
S   Convent
WINDSOR
ASHTON
ASHTO
RICHMOND
PK
FAIRY HILL
MOUNT
ALBANY
SPRINGHILL
BROOKVILLE
PARK
ROCKFORD GDN.
WINDSOR DR.
MONKS
Sports Grd.
ABBEY

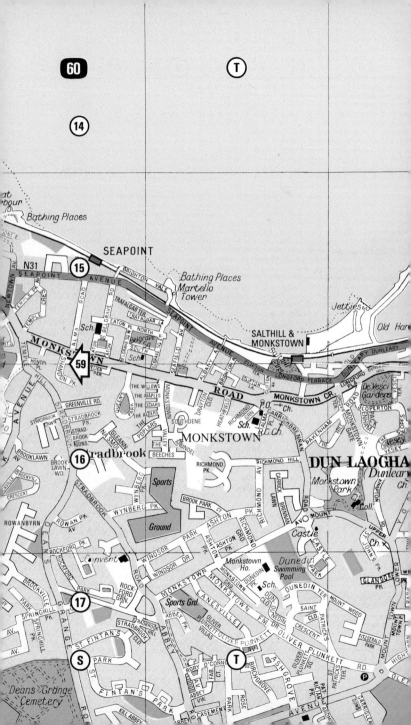

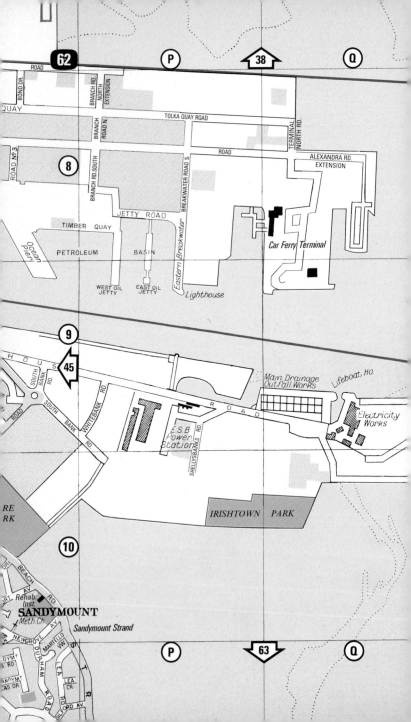

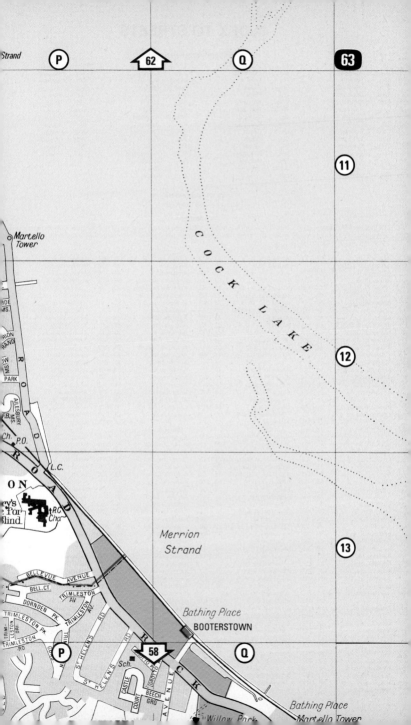

Strand

P   62   Q   **63**

11

○ *Martello Tower*

C O C K   L A K E

12

Merrion Strand

13

Bathing Place
BOOTERSTOWN

P   58   Q

Bathing Place
Martello Tower

Sch.

INDEX TO STREETS

General Abbreviations

All.	Alley	Ex.	Exchange	Lo.	Lodge	Sch.	School
Av.	Avenue	Ext.	Extension	Lwr.	Lower	Sq.	Square
Bk.	Bank	Fld.	Field	Mans.	Mansions	St.	Street
Bldgs.	Buildings	Flds.	Fields	Mkt.	Market	Sta.	Station
Boul.	Boulevard	Fm.	Farm	Ms.	Mews	Ter.	Terrace
Bri.	Bridge	Gdn.	Garden	Mt.	Mount	Vill.	Villa
Cem.	Cemetery	Gdns.	Gardens	N.	North	Vills.	Villas
Ch.	Church	Gra.	Grange	No.	Numbers	Vw.	View
Clo.	Close	Grd.	Ground	Par.	Parade	W.	West
Coll.	College	Grn.	Green	Pas.	Passage	Wd.	Wood
Cotts.	Cottages	Gro.	Grove	Pk.	Park	Wds.	Woods
Cres.	Crescent	Ho.	House	Pl.	Place	Wk.	Walk
Ct.	Court	Hosp.	Hospital	Prom.	Promenade	Yd.	Yard
Dr.	Drive	Hts.	Heights	Rd.	Road		
E.	East	Junct.	Junction	Ri.	Rise		
Est.	Estate	La.	Lane	S.	South		

District Abbreviations

D.L.   Dún Laoghaire

Notes

This index contains some street names in standard text which are followed by another street named in italics. In these cases the stree in standard text does not actually appear on the map due to insufficient space but can be located close to the street named in italics

Street			
Abbey Cotts. 1	43	K8	
Abbey St. Upper			
Abbey Ct. 5	26	P4	
Abbey Pk. 5	25	O4	
Abbey Pk., Baldoyle	28	U2	
Abbey Pk., D.L.	60	T17	
Abbey Rd., D.L.	60	T17	
Abbey St., Howth	31	BB3	
Abbey St. Lwr.	43	K8	
Abbey St. Middle 1	43	K8	
Abbey St. Old 1	44	L8	
Abbey St. Upper 1	43	K8	
Abbey Theatre 1	44	L8	
Abbey St. Old			
Abbey Vw., D.L.	60	T17	
Abbey Vw. Lo., D.L.	60	T17	
Abbeyfield 5	26	P4	
Abbeyfield 6	50	L13	
Abbotstown Av. 11	21	E3	
(Ascal Bhaile An Abba)			
Abbotstown Dr. 11	21	E2	
Abbotstown Rd. 11	21	F2	
Abercorn Rd. 3	44	M8	
Abercorn Sq. 8	41	E9	
Abercorn Ter. 7	34	H7	
Abercorn Ter. 8	41	E9	
Aberdeen St. 7	42	G8	
Achill Rd. 9	36	L5	
Acres Rd. 8	33	E7	
Adair 4	51	N11	
Adam Ct. 2	43	K9	
Grafton St.			
Adare Av. 5	25	O2	
Adare Dr. 5	26	P2	
Adare Grn. 5	26	P2	
Adare Pk. 5	26	P2	
Adare Rd. 5	26	P2	
Addison Pl. 9	35	K5	
Addison Rd. 3	36	M6	
Addison Ter. 9	35	K5	
Adelaide Ms. 4	63	P12	
Adelaide Rd. 2	43	K10	
Adelaide Rd., D.L.	61	W17	
Adelaide St., D.L.	61	V16	
Adelaide Ter. 8	42	G9	
Brookfield St.			
Adrian Av. 6	48	H12	
Aideen Av. 6	48	G13	
Aideen Dr. 6	48	H13	
Aideen Pl. 6	48	H13	
Aifield Ct. 4	51	N13	
Aikenhead Ter. 4	45	N9	
Ailesbury 9	24	L2	
Ailesbury Dr. 4	51	N12	
Ailesbury Gdns. 4	51	O12	
Ailesbury Gro. 4	51	N12	
Ailesbury Ms. 4	63	P12	
Ailesbury Pk. 4	51	O12	
Ailesbury Rd. 4	51	N12	

Street			
Airfield Pk. 4	51	N13	
Airfield Rd. 6	49	J13	
Albany Av., D.L.	60	T16	
Albany Rd. 6	50	L12	
Albert Coll. Av. 9	23	K3	
Albert Coll. Cres. 9	23	K3	
Albert Coll. Dr. 9	23	K3	
Albert Coll. Lawn 9	23	K3	
Albert Coll. Pk. 9	23	K3	
Albert Coll. Ter. 9	23	K3	
Albert Ct., D.L.	61	W17	
Albert Ct. E. 2	44	M9	
Albert Pk., D.L.	61	W17	
Albert Pl. 8	41	F9	
Inchicore Rd.			
Albert Pl. E. 2	44	M9	
Albert Pl. W. 2	43	K10	
Albert Rd., D.L.	61	W17	
Albert Ter. 2	43	K10	
Albert Pl. W.			
Albert Vills. 4	50	M11	
Morehampton Rd.			
Albion Ter. 8	41	F9	
Inchicore Rd.			
Aldborough Par. 1	36	M7	
Aldborough Pl. 1	36	L7	
Aldborough Sq. 1	36	L7	
Alden Dr., Kilbarrack	28	T3	
Alden Pk., Kilbarrack	28	U2	
Alden Rd., Kilbarrack	28	T3	
Alders, The, D.L.	60	T16	
Aldrin Wk. 5	25	O2	
Alexander Ter. 1	45	N8	
Alexander Ter. 8	49	J11	
Alexandra Quay 1	45	O8	
Alexandra Rd. 1	45	N8	
Alexandra Rd. Ext. 1	62	Q8	
Alexandra Ter. 3	38	Q7	
Clontarf Rd.			
Alexandra Ter. 6	49	J13	
Alexandra Ter.	56	M16	
(Dundrum) 14			
Alfie Byrne Rd. 3	37	N7	
All Hallows Coll. 9	36	L5	
All Hallows La. 9	36	L5	
Drumcondra Rd. Upper			
All Saints Dr. 5	27	R4	
All Saints Pk. 5	27	R4	
All Saints Rd. 5	27	R4	
Allen Pk. Rd.,	58	P16	
Stillorgan			
Allingham St. 8	42	H9	
Alma Pl., D.L.	60	T16	
Alma Rd., D.L.	59	S15	
Almeida Av. 8	42	G9	
Brookfield St.			
Almeida Ter. 8	42	G9	
Brookfield St.			
Alone Wk. 5	26	P4	

Street			
Altona Ter. 7	34	H7	
Alverno 3	37	O6	
Amiens St. 1	44	L8	
Anglesea Av., D.L.	59	R15	
Anglesea Fruit Mkt. 7	43	J8	
Green St. Little			
Anglesea La., D.L.	61	V16	
Anglesea Rd. 4	51	N12	
Anglesea Row 7	43	K8	
Anglesea St. 2	43	K9	
Anna Vill. 6	50	L12	
Annadale Av. 3	36	M6	
Annadale Cres. 9	36	M5	
Annadale Dr. 9	36	M5	
Annaly Rd. 7	34	H6	
Annamoe Dr. 7	34	H7	
Annamoe Par. 7	34	H7	
Annamoe Pk. 7	34	H7	
Annamoe Rd. 7	34	H6	
Annamoe Ter. 7	34	H7	
Annaville Gro. 14	56	M15	
Annaville Pk. 14	56	L15	
Annaville Ter. 14	56	M15	
Annaville Gro.			
Anne Devlin Av. 14	54	G16	
Anne Devlin Dr. 14	54	G16	
Anne Devlin Pk. 14	54	G16	
Anne Devlin Rd. 14	54	G16	
Anne St. N. 7	43	J8	
Anne St. S. 2	43	K9	
Anner Rd. 8	41	F9	
Annes La. 2	43	K9	
Annesley Av. 3	36	M7	
Annesley Bri. 3	36	M6	
Annesley Bri. Rd. 3	36	M6	
Annesley Pk. 6	50	L12	
Annesley Pl. 3	36	M7	
Annsbrook 14	56	M14	
Appian Way, The 6	50	L11	
Aranleigh Mt. 14	55	J16	
Aranleigh Mt. Ct. 14	55	J16	
Aranleigh Mt. Pk. 14	55	J16	
Aranleigh Mt. 14	54	H16	
Arbour Hill 7	42	H8	
Arbour Pl. 7	42	H8	
Arbour Ter. 7	42	H8	
Arbutus Av. 12	49	J11	
Arbutus Pl. 8	43	J10	
Arcade 1	43	K8	
Ard Rí Pl. 7	42	H8	
Ard Rí Rd.			
Ard Rí Rd. 7	42	H8	
Ardagh Rd. 12	48	G11	
Ardbeg Cres. 5	26	P3	
Ardbeg Dr. 5	26	P3	
Ardbeg Pk. 5	26	P3	
Ardbeg Rd. 5	26	P3	
Ardcollum Av. 5	26	P3	
Ardee Gro. 6	49	K11	

Street			
Ardee Rd. 6	49	K11	
Ardee Row 8	43	J1	
Ardee St. 8	43	J1	
Ardenza Pk., D.L.	59	S1	
Seapoint Av.			
Ardenza Ter., D.L.	59	S1	
Ardilaun Rd. 3	36	M	
Ballybough Rd.			
Ardilea Downs 14	57	N1	
Ardlea Rd. 5	25	O	
Ardmore Av. 7	34	H	
Ardmore Clo. 5	25	N	
Ardmore Cres. 5	25	O	
Ardmore Dr. 5	25	O	
Ardmore Gro. 5	25	N	
Ardmore Pk. 5	25	O	
Ardmore Pk., D.L.	60	T1	
Ardpatrick Rd. 7	33	F	
Ardtona Av. 14	56	L1	
Argyle Rd. 4	50	M1	
Arklow St. 7	34	H	
Ascal Bhaile Thuaidh	21	R	
(Ballyhoy Av.) 5			
Ascal Dun Eanna	26	O	
(Ennafort Av.) 5			
Ascal Mac Amhlaoi	26	O	
(McAuley Av.) 5			
Ascal Measc	26	P	
(Mask Av.) 5			
Ascal Phairc An	33	F	
Bhailtini 7			
(Villa Pk. Av.)			
Ascal Ratabhachta	21	E	
(Ratoath Av.) 11			
Asgard Pk., Howth	31	BB	
Asgard Rd., Howth	31	BB	
Ash St. 8	43	J	
Ashbrook 3	37	O	
Ashbrook,	32	D	
Castleknock			
Ashcroft 5	27	R	

64

Name	Pg	Grid	Name	Pg	Grid	Name	Pg	Grid	Name	Pg	Grid
hdale Av. 6	48	H13	Baggot Rd. 7	33	E6	Bath Av. Gdns. 4	45	N10	Belgrave Sq. S. 6	49	K12
hdale Gdns. 6	48	H13	Baggot St. Lwr. 2	44	L10	Bath Av. Pl. 4	45	N10	Belgrave Sq. S., D.L.	59	S15
hdale Pk. 6	48	H13	Baggot St. Upper 4	44	M10	Bath La. 1	35	K7	Belgrave Sq. W. 6	49	K12
hfield Av. 6	50	L12	Baggot Ter. 7	33	E6	Bath Pl., D.L.	59	R15	Belgrave Sq. W., D.L.	59	S15
hfield Clo. 6	53	F15	*Blackhorse Av.*			Bath St. 4	45	N9	Belgrave Ter., D.L.	59	S15
hfield Pk. Templeogue) 6	53	F15	Bailey Grn. Rd., Howth	31	BB4	Baymount Pk. 3	39	R6	*Belgrave Rd.*		
Ashfield Rd. Terenure) 6	48	H13	Baldoyle Rd., Baldoyle	29	W2	Bayside Boul. N., Kilbarrack	28	U2	Belgrove Lawn, Chapelizod	40	C8
hfield Rd. (Ranelagh) 6	50	L12	Balfe Av. 12	47	E12	Bayside Boul. S., Kilbarrack	28	U3	Belgrove Pk., Chapelizod	40	C8
hfield Rd. Templeogue) 6	53	F15	Balfe Rd. 12	47	E12	Bayside Pk., Kilbarrack	28	U2	Belgrove Rd. 3	38	P7
hford Cotts. 7	34	H7	Balfe Rd. E. 12	47	E12	Bayside Sq. E., Kilbarrack	29	U2	Bella Av. 1	36	L7
hford Pl. 7	34	H7	Balfe St. 2	43	K9	Bayside Sq. N., Kilbarrack	29	U2	*Bella St.*		
hford St. 7	34	H7	*Chatham St.*			Bayside Sq. S., Kilbarrack	29	U3	Bella St. 1	36	L7
hgrove, D.L.	60	T17	Balglass Est., Howth	31	AA3	Bayside Sq. W., Kilbarrack	29	U3	Belle Bk. 8	42	H9
hington Av. 7	33	E5	Balglass Rd., Howth	31	BB3	Bayside Sta., Kilbarrack	29	V2	Belleville Av. 6	49	J13
hington Clo. 7	33	E5	Balkill Pk., Howth	31	AA3	Bayside Wk., Kilbarrack	28	U2	Bellevue 8	42	H9
hington Ct. 7	33	E5	Balkill Rd., Howth	31	BB3	Bayview 4	45	N9	Bellevue Av. 4	63	P13
hington Dale 7	33	F5	Ballsbridge Av. 4	51	N11	*Pembroke St.*			Bellevue Copse, D.L.	63	P13
hington Gdns. 7	33	F5	Ballsbridge Pk. 4	51	N11	Bayview Av. 3	36	M7	Bellevue Ct., D.L.	63	P13
hington Grn. 7	33	F5	Ballsbridge Ter. 4	51	N11	Beach Av. 4	45	O10	Bellevue Pk., Stillorgan	63	P13
hington Ms. 7	33	F5	*Ballsbridge Av.*			Beach Dr. 4	45	O10	Bellevue Pk. Av., D.L.	63	P13
hington Pk. 7	33	E5	Ballsbridge Wd. 4	45	N10	Beach Rd. 4	45	O10	Bellmans Wk. 1	44	M8
hington Ri. 7	33	E5	Ballyboggan Rd. 11	21	F4	Beach Vw., Howth	28	U3	*Ferrymans Crossing*		
hling Clo. 12	48	G11	Ballybough Av. 3	36	M7	Beaconsfield Ct. 8	41	F9	Belmont Av. 4	50	M12
hton Pk., D.L.	60	T16	*Spring Gdn. St.*			*The Belfry*			Belmont Ct. 4	50	M12
htown Gate Rd. 8	32	D5	Ballybough Bri. 3	36	M6	Beattys Av. 4	51	N11	*Belmont Av.*		
htown Gro. 7	33	E5	Ballybough Ct. 3	36	M7	Beaufield Manor, D.L.	58	P16	Belmont Gdns. 4	50	M12
htown Rd., Castleknock	32	D5	*Spring Gdn. St.*			Beaufield Pk., Stillorgan	58	P16	Belmont Pk. 4	50	M12
htown Sta., Ashtown	20	D4	Ballybough Rd. 3	36	M7	Beaufort, D.L.	61	W17	Belmont Pk. 5	27	S3
ton Pl. 2	43	K8	Ballyfermot Av. 10	40	C9	Beaufort Downs 14	54	H16	Belmont Vills. 4	50	M12
ton Quay 2	43	K8	Ballyfermot Cres. 10	40	C9	Beaumont Av. 14	56	L16	Belton Pk. Av. 9	25	N4
lumney Vills. 6	49	K11	Ballyfermot Par. 10	40	C9	Beaumont Clo. 14	55	K16	Belton Pk. Gdns. 9	25	N4
burn Av. 4	50	M12	Ballygall Av. 11	22	H2	Beaumont Cres. 9	25	N3	Belton Pk. Rd. 9	25	N4
burn Rd. 4	50	M12	Ballygall Cres. 11	22	G3	Beaumont Dr. 14	56	L16	Belton Pk. Vills. 9	25	N4
Auburn Av.			Ballygall Par. 11	22	G3	Beaumont Gdns., D.L.	58	Q15	Belvedere Av. 1	36	L7
burn St. 7	35	J7	Ballygall Pl. 11	22	H3	Beaumont Gro. 9	24	M3	Belvidere Pl. 1	35	K7
burn Vills. 6	49	J13	Ballygall Rd. E. 11	23	J3	Beaumont Rd. 9	24	M4	Belvidere Rd. 1	35	K7
burn Wk. 7	34	H7	Ballygall Rd. W. 11	22	G3	Beauvale Pk. 5	25	O3	Belview Bldgs. 8	42	H9
dilaun Rd. 3	36	L7	Ballygihen Av., D.L.	61	W17	Beaver Row 4	50	M13	*School St.*		
ghavanagh Rd. 12	48	H11	Ballyhoy Av. 5	27	R4	Beaver St. 1	44	L8	Ben Edar Rd. 7	34	H7
ghrim La. 7	34	H7	(Ascal Bhaile Thuaidh)			Bedford Row 2	43	K9	Ben Inagh Pk., Booterstown	59	R14
ghrim Pl. 7	34	H7	Ballymace Grn. 14	53	F16	*Temple Bar*			Benbulbin Av. 12	47	F11
ghrim St. 7	34	H7	Ballymount Dr. 12	46	C13	Beech Gro., D.L.	58	Q14	Benbulbin Rd. 12	41	F10
ghrim Vills. 7	34	H7	Ballymun Rd. 9	23	K4	Beech Hill 4	50	M13	Benburb St. 7	42	H8
Aughrim St.			Ballyneety Rd. 10	40	D9	Beech Hill Av. 4	51	N13	Beneavin Ct. 11	23	J3
ngier Pl. 2	43	K9	Ballyroan Cres. 14	54	G16	Beech Hill Cres. 4	51	N13	Beneavin Dr. 11	23	J3
ngier St. 2	43	K9	Ballyroan Hts. 14	54	G16	Beech Hill Dr. 4	51	N13	Beneavin Pk. 11	22	H2
stins Cotts. 6	36	M7	Ballyroan Pk. 14	53	F16	Beech Hill Ter. 4	51	N13	Beneavin Rd. 11	22	H2
Annesley Pl.			Ballyroan Rd. 14	53	F16	Beech Hill Vills. 4	51	N13	Bengal Ter. 9	35	J5
e Maria Rd. 8	42	H10	Ballyshannon Av. 5	25	N2	*Beech Hill Ter.*			Benmadigan Rd. 12	41	F10
enue, The 12	53	F15	Ballyshannon Rd. 5	25	N2	Beech Pk. Av. 5	26	P2	Benson St. 2	45	N9
enue Rd. 8	49	J11	Ballytore Rd. 14	55	J14	Beechdale Ms. 6	49	K12	Beresford 9	36	L5
oca Av., D.L.	58	Q15	Balnagowan 6	50	L12	Beeches, The 5	27	S2	Beresford Av. 9	36	L5
oca Pk., Stillorgan	58	Q15	Balscadden Rd., Howth	31	BB3	Beeches, The, D.L.	60	T16	Beresford La. 1	44	L8
oca Pl., D.L.	59	R15	Bancroft Clo., Tallaght	52	C16	Beechfield Av. 12	47	E13	Beresford La. 9	36	L5
oca Rd., D.L.	58	Q16	Bancroft Gro., Tallaght	52	C16	Beechfield Clo. 12	47	E13	Beresford Pl. 1	44	L8
ondale Av. 7	35	J7	Bancroft Rd., Tallaght	52	C16	Beechfield Rd. 12	47	E13	Beresford St. 7	43	J8
ondale Ct., D.L.	61	W17	Bangor Dr. 12	48	G11	Beechlawn, D.L.	58	P15	Berkeley Rd. 7	35	K7
ondale Lawn, D.L.	59	R16	Bangor Rd. 12	48	G11	Beechmount Dr. 14	56	M14	Berkeley St. 7	35	K7
ondale Lawn Ext., D.L.	59	R16	Bank of Ireland 2	43	K9	Beechwood Av. Lwr. 6	50	L12	Berkeley Ter. 4	45	N10
ondale Pk. 5	27	S4	Bankside Cotts. 14	56	L14	Beechwood Av. Upper 6	50	L12	Berryfield Cres. 11	21	F4
ondale Rd. 7	35	J7	Bann Rd. 11	34	G5	Beechwood Gro., D.L.	61	V17	Berryfield Dr. 11	21	F4
ondale Ter. 12	47	E13	Bannow Rd. 7	34	G5	Beechwood Ms. 6	49	K12	Berryfield Rd. 11	21	F3
refield Av. 5	26	Q2	Bantry Rd. 9	23	K4	Beechwood Pk., D.L.	61	V17	Berwick Hall 14	55	J16
refield Ct. 5	26	Q2	Barclay Ct., D.L.	59	R15	Beechwood Rd. 6	50	L12	Berystede 6	50	L11
refield Dr. 5	26	Q2	Bargy Rd. 3	37	N7	Belfield Clo. 14	56	M14	*Leeson Pk.*		
refield Gro. 5	26	Q2	Barnamore Cres. 11	22	G4	Belfield Ct. 4	51	N13	Bessborough Av. 3	36	M7
refield Pl. 5	26	Q2	*Barnamore Gro.*			Belfield Downs 14	56	M15	Bessborough Par. 6	49	K11
			Barnamore Gro. 11	22	G4	Belfry, The 8	41	F9	Bethesda Pl. 1	35	K7
B			Barnamore Pk. 11	22	G4	Belgrave Av. 6	49	K12	*Dorset St. Upper*		
chelors Wk. 1	43	K8	Barrett St., D.L.	60	U16	Belgrave Pl. 6	49	K12	Bettyglen 5	28	T4
ck La. 8	43	J9	Barrow Rd. 11	34	H5	Belgrave Rd. 6	49	K12	Bettystown Av. 5	27	R4
ggot Clo. 2	44	L10	Barrow St. 4	44	M9	Belgrave Sq. E. 6	49	K12	Big Bri. 6	54	H14
Baggot La. Lwr.			Barry Av. 11	21	F2	Belgrave Sq. E., D.L.	60	T15	Biggar Rd. 12	47	E12
ggot Ct. 2	44	L10	Barry Dr. 11	21	F2	Belgrave Sq. N. 6	49	K12	Binn Eadair Vw., Sutton	29	W2
ggot La. 4	44	M10	Barry Grn. 11	21	F2	Belgrave Sq. N., D.L.	59	S15	Binns Bri. 1	35	K6
			Barry Pk. 11	21	F2				Birchfield 14	57	N16
			Barry Rd. 11	21	F2				Birchgrove, D.L.	60	T17
			Barryscourt Rd. 5	25	O2				Birchs La. 14	56	M16
			Barton Av. 14	54	H16				Bird Av. 14	56	M14
			Barton Dr. 14	54	H16				Bishop St. 8	43	K10
			Basin St. Lwr. 8	42	H9				Black Pitts 8	43	J10
			Basin St. Upper 8	42	H9				Black St. 7	42	G8
			Basin Vw. Ter. 7	35	K7				Blackberry La. 6	49	K11
			Bass Pl. 2	44	L9				Blackhall Par. 7	43	J8
			Bath Av. 4	45	N10						

Name	Page	Grid
Blackhall Pl. 7	42	H8
Blackhall St. 7	43	J8
Blackheath Av. 3	38	Q6
Blackheath Dr. 3	38	P6
Blackheath Gdns. 3	38	P6
Blackheath Gro. 3	38	P6
Blackheath Pk. 3	38	P6
Blackhorse Av. 7	32	D5
Blackhorse Bri. 8	41	E10
Blackhorse Gro. 7	34	H7
Blackrock Coll., D.L.	58	Q14
Blackrock Sta., D.L.	59	R14
Blackwater Rd. 11	34	H5
Blarney Pk. 12	48	G12
Blessington Ct. 7	35	K7
Blessington St.		
Blessington St. 7	35	K7
Bloom Cotts. 8	43	J10
Bloomfield Av.	50	L11
(Donnybrook) 4		
Bloomfield Av.	43	J10
(Portobello) 8		
Bloomfield Pk. 8	49	J11
Bluebell Av. 12	46	D11
Bluebell Rd. 12	46	D11
Blythe Av. 3	44	M8
Church Rd.		
Boden Wd. 14	54	H16
Bolton St. 1	43	K8
Bon Secours Hosp. 9	23	K4
Bond Dr. 1	45	O8
Bond Rd. 1	45	N8
Bond St. 8	42	H9
Bonham St. 8	42	H9
Boolavogue Rd. 3	36	M7
Booterstown Av., D.L.	58	P15
Booterstown Pk., D.L.	58	P15
Booterstown Sta., Booterstown	63	Q13
Botanic Av. 9	35	K5
Botanic Gdns. 11	35	J5
Botanic Ms. 9	35	J5
Botanic Pk. 9	35	K5
Botanic Rd. 9	35	J6
Botanic Vills. 9	35	K5
Botanic Rd.		
Bothar Ainninn (Ennel Rd.) 5	26	Q3
Bothar An Easa (Watermill Rd.) 5	27	R4
Bothar Cloiche Na Manac 12 (Walkinstown Rd.)	46	D12
Bothar Coilbeard (Con Colbert Rd.) 8	41	E9
Bothar Dhroichead Chiarduibh 11 (Cardiffsbridge Rd.)	21	F3
Bothar Phairc An Bhailtini 7 (Villa Pk. Rd.)	33	F6
Bothar Raitleann (Rathland Rd.) 12	48	G13
Boundary Rd. 1	37	O7
Bow Bri. 8	42	G9
Bow La. E. 2	43	K9
Bow La. W. 8	42	G9
Bow St. 7	43	J8
Boyne La. 2	44	L9
Boyne Rd. 11	34	G5
Boyne St. 2	44	L9
Brabazon Row 8	43	J10
Brabazon Sq. 8	43	J9
Pimlico		
Brabazon St. 8	43	J9
The Coombe		
Brackens La. 2	44	L8
Braemor Av. 14	55	K15
Braemor Dr. 14	55	K15
Braemor Gro. 14	55	K15
Braemor Pk. 14	55	K14
Braemor Rd. 14	55	K15
Brainborough Ter. 8	42	H10
South Circular Rd.		
Braithwaite St. 8	42	H9
Brakens La. 2	44	L8
Moss St.		
Branch Rd. N. 1	62	P8
Branch Rd. N. Ext. 1	62	P8
Branch Rd. S. 1	62	P8
Brandon Rd. 12	47	E11
Breakwater Rd. S. 1	62	P8
Bregia Rd. 7	34	H6
Bremen Av. 4	45	O10
Bremen Gro. 4	45	O9
Bremen Rd. 4	45	O9
Brendan Behan Ct. 1	36	L7
Russell St.		
Brendan Dr. (Ceide Brendain) 5	26	P3
Brendan Rd. 4	50	M12
Brian Av. 3	36	M5
Brian Boru Av. 3	38	Q7
Brian Boru St. 3	38	Q7
Brian Rd. 3	36	M6
Brian Ter. 3	36	M6
Briarfield Gro. 5	28	T3
Briarfield Rd. 5	27	S3
Briarfield Vills. 5	28	T3
Brickfield Dr. 12	42	G10
Brickfield La. 8	42	H10
Bride Rd. 8	43	J9
Bride St. 8	43	J9
Bride St. New 8	43	K10
Bridge St. 4	45	N9
Bridge St. Lwr. 8	43	J9
Bridge St. Upper 8	43	J9
Bridgefoot St. 8	43	J9
Bridgewater Quay 8	41	F9
Brighton Av. 3	37	N6
Brighton Av. 6	49	J13
Brighton Av., D.L.	60	T16
Brighton Gdns. 6	49	J13
Brighton Grn. 6	49	J13
Brighton Rd. 6	49	J13
Brighton Sq. 6	49	J13
Brighton Vale, D.L.	59	S15
Britain Pl. 1	43	K8
Britain Quay 2	45	N9
Broadstone 7	35	J7
Broadstone Av. 7	35	J7
Phibsborough Rd.		
Brodin Row 7	42	H8
Brook Pk. Ct., D.L.	60	T16
Brookfield 6	50	L13
Brookfield, D.L.	58	Q15
Brookfield Av. 5	26	Q3
Brookfield Est. 12	46	D11
Brookfield Pl., D.L.	59	R15
Brookfield Rd. 8	42	G9
Brookfield St. 8	42	G9
Brookfield Ter., D.L.	59	R15
Brooklands	51	O12
Brooklawn 3	37	O6
Brooklawn, D.L.	58	Q15
Brooklawn Av., D.L.	59	S16
Brooklawn Wd., D.L.	59	S16
Brookmount Av., Tallaght	52	D16
Brookmount Lawn, Tallaght	52	D16
Tallaght Rd.		
Brookvale Downs 14	54	H14
Brookvale Rd. 4	50	M12
Brookvale Rd. 14	54	H15
Brookville 11	22	G2
Brookville Cres. 5	26	P2
Brookville Pk. 5	26	P3
Brookville Pk., D.L.	60	S17
Brookwood Av. 5	26	P4
Brookwood Cres. 5	26	Q4
Brookwood Dr. 5	26	Q4
Brookwood Glen 5	26	Q4
Brookwood Gro. 5	26	Q4
Brookwood Hts. 5	26	P4
Brookwood Lawn 5	26	Q4
Brookwood Meadow 5	26	P4
Brookwood Pk. 5	26	Q4
Brookwood Ri. 5	26	Q4
Brookwood Rd. 5	26	P4
Broombridge Rd. 7	34	G5
Broombridge Sta. 7	34	G5
Brown St. N. 7	43	J8
Brown St. S. 8	42	H10
Brunswick Pl. 2	44	M9
Pearse St.		
Brunswick St. N. 7	43	J8
Brusna Cotts., D.L.	59	R15
Buckingham St. Lwr. 1	36	L7
Buckingham St. Upper 1	36	L7
Bulfin Gdns. 8	41	F9
Bulfin Rd. 8	41	F9
Bulfin St. 8	41	F10
Bull All. St. 8	43	J9
Bunratty Av. 5	26	P2
Bunratty Dr. 5	26	P2
Bunratty Rd. 5	25	O2
Bunting Rd. 12	46	D12
Burdett Av., D.L.	61	W17
Burgess La. 7	43	J8
Haymarket		
Burgh Quay 2	43	K8
Burke Pl. 8	42	G9
Burleigh Ct. 4	50	L11
Burlington Gdns. 4	44	L10
Burlington Rd. 4	44	L10
Burris Ct. 8	43	J9
School Ho. La. W.		
Burrow Rd., Howth	30	X2
Burrowfield Rd., Baldoyle	29	W2
Bushfield Av. 4	50	M12
Bushfield Pl. 4	50	L12
Bushfield Ter. 4	50	L12
Bushy Pk. Gdns. 6	55	J14
Bushy Pk. Rd. 6	54	H14
Butterfield Av. 14	53	F16
Butterfield Clo. 14	54	G16
Butterfield Cres. 14	54	H15
Butterfield Dr. 14	54	H16
Butterfield Gro. 14	54	G16
Butterfield Orchard 14	54	H16
Butterfield Pk. 14	54	G16
Byrnes La. 1	43	K8

C

Name	Page	Grid
Cabra Dr. 7	34	H6
Cabra Gro. 7	34	H6
Cabra Pk. 7	35	J6
Cabra Rd. 7	34	G6
Cadogan Rd. 3	36	M6
Calderwood Av. 9	24	M4
Calderwood Gro. 9	36	M5
Calderwood Rd. 9	36	M5
Caledon Rd. 3	36	M7
Callary Rd., Stillorgan	57	O15
Camac Pk. 12	46	C11
Camac Ter. 8	42	G9
Bow La.		
Cambells Ct. 7	43	J8
Little Britain St.		
Camberley Oaks 14	55	K16
Cambridge Av. 4	45	O9
Cambridge La. 6	49	K12
Cambridge Rd. 4	45	N9
Cambridge Rd. (Rathmines) 6	49	K12
Cambridge St. 4	45	N9
Cambridge Ter. 6	50	L11
Cambridge Vills. 6	49	K12
Belgrave Rd.		
Camden Lock 2	45	N9
South Docks Rd.		
Camden Mkt. 2	43	K10
Camden St. Lwr.		
Camden Pl. 2	43	K10
Camden Row 8	43	K10
Camden St. Lwr. 2	43	K10
Camden St. Upper 2	43	K10
Cameron Sq. 8	42	G9
Cameron St. 8	42	H10
Campbells Row 1	36	L7
Portland St. N.		
Canal Rd. 6	49	K11
Canal Ter. 12	40	D10
Cannon Rock Vw., Howth	31	BB3
Canon Kill Ct. 12	47	F12
Canon Lillis Av. 1	44	M8
Canon Mooney Gdns. 4	45	N9
Cambridge Rd.		
Canon Troy Ct. 10	40	C9
Capel St. 1	43	K8
Cappagh Av. 11	21	F2
Cappagh Dr. 11	21	F3
Cappagh Rd. 11	21	E...
Captains Av. 12	47	F1
Captains Dr. 12	47	F1
Captains Rd. 12	47	F1
Caragh Rd. 7	34	G...
Carberry Rd. 9	36	M...
Cardiff Br. 7	35	J
Phibsborough Rd.		
Cardiff Castle Rd. 11	21	F
Cardiffs La. 2	44	M
Cardiffsbridge Av. 11	21	E
Cardiffsbridge Gro. 11	21	F
Cappagh Rd.		
Cardiffsbridge Rd. 11	21	F
(Bothar Dhroichead Chiarduibh)		
Cards La. 2	44	L
Townsend St.		
Carleton Rd. 3	37	N
Carlingford Par. 2	44	M
Carlingford Pl. 2	44	M
Carlingford Par.		
Carlingford Rd. 9	35	K
Carlisle Av. 4	50	M...
Carlisle St. 8	43	J...
Carlton Ct. 3	37	C
Carlton Ms. 4	45	N...
Shelbourne Av.		
Carmans Hall 8	43	...
Carndonagh Dr. 5	28	T
Carndonagh Lawn 5	28	T
Carndonagh Pk. 5	28	T
Carndonagh Rd. 5	28	T
Carnew St. 7	34	H
Carnlough Rd. 7	34	G
Caroline Row 4	45	N
Bridge St.		
Carraroe Av. 5	27	S
Carrick Brennan Lawn, D.L.	60	T...
Carrick Ter. 8	42	H...
Carrickbrack Heath, Howth	30	...
Carrickbrack Hill, Howth	30	...
Carrickbrack Lawn, Howth	30	...
Carrickbrack Pk., Howth	30	...
Carrickbrack Rd., Howth	30	...
Carrickbrennan Rd., D.L.	60	T...
Carrickmount Av. 14	55	K...
Carrickmount Dr. 14	55	K...
Carrickmount Lawn 14	55	K...
Carrigallen Dr. 11	22	G
Carrigallen Rd.		
Carrigallen Pk. 11	22	...
Carrigallen Rd.		
Carrigallen Rd. 11	22	...
Carrow Rd. 12	41	E
Carysfort Av., D.L.	59	R
Carysfort Hall, D.L.	59	R
Carysfort Pk., Stillorgan	59	R
Casana Vw., Howth	31	BB...
Casement Dr. 11	21	...
Casement Grn. 11	21	...
Casement Gro. 11	21	...
Casement Pk. 11	21	...
Casement Rd. (Finglas S.) 11	22	...
Casement Vills., D.L.	60	T...
Cashel Av. 12	48	G
Cashel Rd. 12	47	F
Casimir Av. 6	49	J
Casimir Ct. 6	49	J
Casimir Rd. 6	48	H
Casino Pk. 9	37	N
Casino Rd. 3	36	N
Castilla Pk. 3	38	...
Castle Av. 3	38	...
Castle Ct. 3	37	N
Castle Ct. 14	55	J...
Castle Ct., D.L.	58	P...
Castle Gate, Castleknock	32	...
Castle Golf Course 14	55	...
Castle Gro. 3	38	...

Castle Lawns, Tallaght 52 C16
Castle Mkt. 2 43 K9
Drury St.
Castle Pk., D.L. 60 T16
Castle Pk. Est., Tallaght 52 C16
Castle Rd. 3 38 P6
Castle St. 2 43 K9
Castlebyrne Pk., Stillorgan 59 R16
Castledawson Av., D.L. 58 Q14
Castleforbes Rd. 1 45 N8
Castlekevin Rd. 5 25 O2
Castlelands, The 14 55 J15
Castlepark Rd., D.L. 61 W17
Castleside Dr. 14 55 J15
Castletimon Av. 5 25 N2
Castletimon Dr. 5 25 N2
Castletimon Gdns. 9 25 N2
Castletimon Grn. 5 25 N2
Castletimon Pk. 5 25 N2
Castletimon Rd. 5 25 N2
Castletymon Ct., Tallaght 52 C15
Castleview 5 25 O4
Castlewood Av. 6 49 K12
Castlewood Clo. 6 49 K12
Castlewood Av.
Castlewood La. 6 49 K12
Castlewood Pk. 6 49 K12
Castlewood Pl. 6 49 K12
Castlewood Ter. 6 49 K12
Cathal Brugha St. 1 43 K8
Cathedral La. 8 43 J10
Cathedral St. 1 43 K8
Cathedral Vw. Ct. 8 43 J10
Cathedral Vw. Wk.
Cathedral Vw. Wk. 8 43 J10
Catherine St. 8 43 J9
Ash St.
Catherines La. 7 43 J8
Church St. Upper
Cavendish Row 1 43 K8
Parnell St.
Ceannt Fort 8 42 G9
Cecil Av. 3 37 N6
Cecilia St. 2 43 K9
Temple La. S.
Cedar Ct. 6 48 H13
Cedar Hall 6 50 M13
Prospect La.
Cedar Pk. 5 27 S2
Cedar Sq., Stillorgan 58 Q16
Cedar Wk. 5 27 S3
Cedarmount Rd., Stillorgan 57 O16
Cedars, The, D.L. 60 T16
Cedarwood Av. 11 22 H2
Cedarwood Clo. 11 23 J2
Cedarwood Grn. 11 22 H2
Cedarwood Gro. 11 22 H2
Cedarwood Pk. 11 22 H2
Cedarwood Ri. 11 22 H2
Ceide Brendain (Brendan Dr.) 5 26 P3
Ceide Dun Eanna (Ennafort Dr.) 5 26 Q4
Ceide Gleannaluinn (Glenaulin Dr.), Chapelizod 40 C8
Ceide Phairc An Bhailtin 7 33 F6
(Villa Pk. Dr.)
Celestine Av. 4 45 N9
Celtic Pk. Av. 9 25 N4
Celtic Pk. Rd. 9 25 N4
Central Mental Hosp. 14 56 M15
Chamber St. 8 43 J10
Chancery La. 8 43 K9
Chancery Pl. 7 43 J8
Chancery St. 7 43 J8
Chanel Av. 5 26 P3
Chanel Gro. 5 26 P2
Chanel Rd. 5 26 P3
Chapel Av. 4 45 N9
Chapel La. 1 43 K8
Chapelizod Ct. 10 40 C8

Chapelizod Hill 10 40 C8
Chapelizod Rd. 8 40 D8
Charlemont 9 37 N5
Charlemont Av., D.L. 61 U16
Charlemont Ct. 2 49 K11
Charlemont Ct. 6 49 K11
Charlemont Gdns. 2 43 K10
Charlemont St.
Charlemont Mall 2 49 K11
Charlemont Par. 3 36 M7
Charlemont Pl. 2 49 K11
Charlemont Rd. 3 37 N6
Charlemont Sq. 2 43 K10
Charlemont St.
Charlemont St. 2 43 K10
Charles La. Great 1 36 L7
Charles St. Great 1 36 L7
Charles St. W. 7 43 J8
Charleston Av. 6 49 K12
Charleston Rd. 6 49 K12
Charleville 14 56 L15
Charleville Av. 3 36 M7
Charleville Mall 1 36 L7
Charleville Rd. 6 49 J12
Charleville Rd. 7 34 H6
Charlotte Quay 4 44 M9
Charlotte St. 2 43 K10
Charlotte Way 2 43 K10
Charlton Lawn 14 57 N15
Chatham Row 2 43 K9
William St. S.
Chatham St. 2 43 K9
Chaworth Ter. 8 43 J9
Hanbury La.
Cheaters La. 2 43 K10
Redmonds Hill
Chelmsford La. 6 50 L11
Chelmsford Rd. 6 50 L11
Chelsea Gdns. 3 38 Q6
Cheltenham Pl. 6 49 K11
Portobello Br.
Cherbury Ct., D.L. 58 P15
Cherbury Gdns., D.L. 58 P15
Cherbury Ms., D.L. 58 P15
Cherry Ct. 6 48 H13
Cherry Garth, Stillorgan 58 P16
Cherry Gro. 12 47 E13
Cherryfield Av. 6 50 L12
Cherryfield Av. 12 47 E13
Cherryfield Dr. 12 47 E13
Cherryfield Rd. 12 47 E13
Cherrymount Cres. 9 37 N5
Cherrymount Gro. 9 37 N5
Cherrymount Pk. 7 35 J7
Chester Downs, D.L. 61 V17
Chester Rd. 6 50 L11
Chester Sq., D.L. 61 W17
Chesterfield Av., Castleknock 32 C5
Chesterfield Clo., Castleknock 32 C5
Chesterfield Copse, Castleknock 32 C5
Chesterfield Gro., Castleknock 32 C5
Chesterfield Pk., Castleknock 32 C5
Chesterfield Vw., Castleknock 32 C5
Chestnut Ct. 9 25 N4
Chestnut Rd., Stillorgan 57 O15
Christ Ch. Cathedral 8 43 J9
Christchurch Pl. 8 43 J9
Church Av. (Irishtown) 4 45 O10
Church Av. (Harolds-cross) 6 43 J10
Church Av. (Rathmines) 6 49 K12
Church Av. (Rialto) 8 42 G10
Church Av. (Glasnevin) 9 23 K4
Church Av. N. (Drumcondra) 9 36 L5
Church Dr. 6 48 H12
Church Gdns. 6 49 K12
Church La. 2 43 K9
College Grn.

Church La. (Rathfarnham) 14 54 H15
Church La. S. 8 43 K10
Kevin St. Lwr.
Church Lawn 6 48 H12
Church Pk. Ct. 6 48 H12
Church Rd. 3 44 M8
Church Rd. (Finglas) 11 22 G3
Church Rd., Howth 30 X2
Church St. 7 43 J8
Church St. (Finglas) 11 22 G3
Church St., Howth 31 AA2
Church St. E. 3 44 M8
Church St. New 7 43 J8
Church St. Upper 7 43 J8
Church Ter. 7 43 J8
Church St.
Church Vw. 6 48 H12
Church Way 6 48 H12
Churchfields 14 56 M14
Churchgate Av. 3 38 Q7
Churchill Ter. 4 51 N11
Churchtown Av. 14 56 L14
Churchtown Clo. 14 56 L14
Churchtown Dr. 14 56 L14
Churchtown Rd. 14 56 K15
Churchtown Rd. Upper 14 56 L14
Cian Pk. 9 36 L6
Cill Eanna 5 27 R4
City Quay 2 44 L8
Clanawley Rd. 5 38 P5
Clanboy Rd. 5 25 O4
Clanbrassil Clo. 12 49 J11
Clanbrassil St. Lwr. 8 49 J11
Clanbrassil St. Upper 8
Clancarthy Rd. 5 37 O5
Clancy Av. 11 22 G2
Clancy Barracks 8 42 G8
Clancy Rd. 11 22 H2
Clandonagh Rd. 5 25 O4
Clanhugh Rd. 5 37 O5
Clanmahon Rd. 5 37 O5
Clanmaurice Rd. 5 26 O4
Clanmoyle Rd. 5 37 O5
Clanranald Rd. 5 25 O4
Clanree Rd. 5 25 O4
Clanwilliam Pl. 2 44 M10
Clare La. 2 44 L9
Clare Rd. 9 36 L5
Clare St. 2 44 L9
Claremont Av. 9 23 K4
Claremont Ct. 11 34 H5
Claremont Dr. 11 23 J3
Claremont Pk. (Pairc Clearmont) 4 45 O10
Claremont Rd. 4 45 O10
Claremont Rd., Howth 30 Y2
Claremont Vills., D.L. 61 V17
Clarence Mangan Rd. 8 43 J10
Clarence St., D.L. 60 U15
Clarendon Mkt. 2 43 K9
Chatham St.
Clarendon Row 2 43 K9
Clarendon St.
Clarendon St. 2 43 K9
Clareville Ct. 11 35 J5
Clareville Gro. 11 35 J5
Clareville Rd. 11 35 J5
Clareville Rd. 6 48 H12
Clarinda Manor, D.L. 61 V17
Clarinda Pk. E., D.L. 61 V17
Clarinda Pk. N., D.L. 61 V16
Clarinda Pk. W., D.L. 61 V17
Clarke Ter. 8 42 H10
Classons Bri. 14 56 L14
Claude Rd. 9 35 K6
Clifton Av., D.L. 60 T16
Clifton La., D.L. 60 T16
Clifton Ms., D.L. 49 K11
Clifton Ter., D.L. 60 T16
Cliftonville Rd. 9 35 K5
Clinches Ct. 3 36 M7
Clogher Rd. 12 48 G11
Cloister Av., Stillorgan 59 R16
Cloister Gate, Stillorgan 59 R16

Cloister Grn., Stillorgan 59 R16
Cloister Gro., Stillorgan 59 R16
Cloister Pk., Stillorgan 58 Q16
Cloister Sq., Stillorgan 59 R16
Cloister Way, Stillorgan 59 R16
Cloisters, The 6 48 H13
Clonard Rd. 12 47 F11
Clonfert Rd. 12 48 G12
Clonlara Rd. 4 45 O9
Clonliffe Av. 3 36 L6
Clonliffe Gdns. 3 36 L6
Clonliffe Rd. 3 36 L6
Clonmacnoise Gro. 12 48 G12
Clonmacnoise Rd. 12 48 G12
Clonmel Rd. 11 23 J3
Clonmel St. 2 43 K10
Clonmore Rd. (Ballybough) 3 36 L7
Clonmore Rd., Stillorgan 57 O16
Clonmore Ter. 3 36 L7
Clonrosse Ct. 5 27 R2
Elton Dr.
Clonrosse Dr. 5 27 R2
Clonrosse Pk. 5 27 R2
Elton Dr.
Clonshaugh Rd. 5 25 O2
Clonskeagh Bri. 6 50 M13
Clonskeagh Castle 14 50 L13
Clonskeagh Rd. 6 50 M12
Clonskeagh Rd. 14 50 M13
Clonskeagh Sq. 14 50 M13
Clontarf Castle 3 38 P6
Clontarf Golf Course 3 37 O5
Clontarf Pk. 3 38 Q7
Clontarf Prom. 3 37 O7
Clontarf Rd. 3 37 N6
Clonturk Av. 9 36 L5
Clonturk Gdns. 9 36 L5
Clonturk Pk. 9 36 L5
Cloonlara Cres. 11 22 G4
Cloonlara Rd.
Cloonlara Dr. 11 22 G4
Cloonlara Rd.
Cloonlara Rd. 11 22 G4
Close, The 6 53 F15
Close, The, Stillorgan 58 P15
Cloyne Rd. 12 48 G12
Club Rd., Walkinstown 46 C12
Clune Rd. 11 22 G2
Clyde La. 4 50 M11
Clyde Rd. 4 50 M11
Coburg Pl. 1 44 M8
Coldwell St., D.L. 61 V17
Colepark Av. 10 40 C9
Colepark Dr. 10 40 C9
Colepark Grn. 10 40 C9
Coleraine St. 7 43 J8
College Cres. 6 53 F14
College Dr. 6 53 G14
College Grn. 2 43 K9
College La. 2 44 L9
Westland Row
College Pk. 6 53 F14
College St. 2 43 K9
Colliers Av. 6 50 L12
Collins Av. 9 24 M4
Collins Av. E. 5 25 O4
Collins Av. Ext. 9 23 K3
Collins Av. W. 9 24 L3
Collins Barracks 7 42 H8
Collins Ct. 9 25 N4
Collins Ct., D.L. 59 R15
Sweetmans Av.
Collins Dr. 11 22 H2
Collins Grn. 11 22 H2
Collins Pk. 9 25 N4
Collins Pl. 11 22 H3
Collins Row 11 22 H3
Collins Wd. 9 24 M4
Comeragh Rd. 12 47 E11
Commons St. 1 44 L8
Con Colbert Rd. 8 41 E9
(Bothar Coilbeard)
Congress Gdns., D.L. 61 W17

Connaught St. 7	35	J6
Connaught Ter. 6	49	J13
Rathgar Rd.		
Connolly Av. 8	41	F9
Connolly Sta. 1	44	L8
Conor Clune Rd. 7	33	E6
Conquer Hill Rd. 3	38	Q7
Conquer Hill Ter. 3	38	Q6
Constitution Hill 7	43	J8
Convent Av. 3	36	M6
Convent Lands 10	40	C9
Convent La. 14	54	H16
Convent Rd.,	59	R15
Blackrock		
Convent Rd., D.L.	61	U16
Convent Vw. Cotts. 7	33	F5
Conway Ct. 2	44	M9
Macken St.		
Conyngham Rd. 8	41	F8
Cook St. 8	43	J9
Coolamber Pk. 14	53	F16
Coolatree Clo. 9	25	N3
Coolatree Pk. 9	24	M3
Coolatree Rd. 9	25	N3
Cooleen Av. 9	24	M2
Coolevin La. 8	43	J10
Long La.		
Cooley Rd. 12	41	E10
Coolgariff Rd. 9	24	M3
Coolgreena Clo. 9	25	N3
Coolgreena Rd. 9	25	N3
Coolock Av. 5	26	P2
Coolock Clo. 5	26	P2
Coolock Ct. 5	26	P2
Coolock Dr. 5	26	P2
Coolock Grn. 5	26	P2
Coolock Gro. 5	26	P2
Coolock Village 5	26	P3
Coolrua Dr. 9	24	M3
Coombe, The 8	43	J9
Cope St. 2	43	K9
Copeland Av. 3	37	N6
Copeland Gro. 3	37	N6
Copper All. 8	43	K9
Coppinger Clo., D.L.	58	Q16
Coppinger Glade,	58	Q16
D.L.		
Coppinger Wk., D.L.	58	Q16
Coppinger Wd., D.L.	58	Q16
Coppingers Row 2	43	K9
William St. S.		
Corballis Row 8	43	J10
Kevin St. Upper		
Cork Hill 2	43	K9
Cork St. 8	42	H10
Cormack Ter. 6	54	H14
Corn Ex. Pl. 2	44	L8
George's Quay		
Cornmarket 8	43	J9
Corporation Bldgs. 8	42	G9
Corporation St. 1	44	L8
Corrib Rd. 6	48	G13
Corrig Av., D.L.	61	V17
Corrig Clo. 12	52	C14
Lugnaquilla Av.		
Corrig Pk., D.L.	61	V17
Corrig Rd., D.L.	61	V17
Corrybeg 12	53	F16
Cottage Pl. 1	35	K6
Portland Pl.		
Coulson Av. 6	49	J13
Coultry Way 9	24	L2
Court, The 3	37	O6
Clontarf Rd.		
Court, The 5	27	S4
Court, The 6	53	F15
Court, The 9	24	M4
Court, The, Sutton	29	W2
Courts of Justice 7	43	J8
Courtyard, The 14	55	J15
Cow Parlour 8	43	J10
Cowbooter La., Howth	31	BB3
Cowley Pl. 7	35	K6
Cowper Downs 6	49	K13
Cowper Dr. 6	50	L13
Cowper Gdns. 6	50	L13
Cowper Rd. 6	49	K13
Cowper St. 7	34	H7
Cowper Village 6	49	K13
Craigford Av. 5	25	O4

Craigford Dr. 5	25	O4
Craigmore Gdns.,	59	S15
D.L.		
Crampton Bldgs. 2	43	K9
Temple Bar		
Crampton Ct. 2	43	K9
Crampton Quay 2	43	K8
Crane La. 2	43	K9
Crane St. 8	42	H9
Cranfield Pl. 4	45	O10
Cranford Ct. 4	51	O13
Cranmer La. 4	44	M10
Crannagh 6	50	M13
Crannagh Castle 14	54	H15
Crannagh Ct. 14	54	H15
Crannagh Gro. 14	55	J14
Crannagh Pk. 14	55	J15
Crannagh Rd. 14	54	H15
Crannagh Way 14	55	J15
Crawford Av. 9	35	K6
Creighton St. 2	44	L9
Cremona Rd. 10	40	C10
Cremore Av. 11	23	J4
Cremore Cres. 11	23	J4
Cremore Dr. 11	23	J4
Cremore Hts. 11	23	J3
Ballygall Rd. E.		
Cremore Lawn 11	23	J4
Cremore Pk. 11	23	J4
Cremore Rd. 11	23	J4
Cremorne 14	53	F16
Crescent, The	50	M12
(Donnybrook) 4		
Crescent, The	24	M3
(Beaumont) 9		
Crescent, The	24	M4
(Whitehall) 9		
Crescent, The, Sutton	29	W2
Crescent Gdns. 3	36	M7
Crescent Pl. 3	37	N6
Crescent Vills. 9	35	K6
Crestfield Av. 9	24	L3
Crestfield Clo. 9	24	L3
Crestfield Dr. 9	24	L3
Crestfield Pk. 9	24	L3
Crestfield Clo.		
Croaghpatrick Rd. 7	33	F6
Crofton Av., D.L.	61	U16
Crofton Rd., D.L.	61	U15
Crofton Ter., D.L.	61	U15
Croker La. 8	42	H9
Cromcastle Av. 5	25	O2
Cromcastle Dr. 5	25	O2
Cromcastle Grn. 5	25	O2
Cromcastle Pk. 5	25	O2
Cromcastle Rd. 5	25	O2
Cromwells Fort Rd. 12	46	D12
Cromwells Quarters 8	42	G9
Cross & Passion	24	M4
Coll. 9		
Cross Av., Blackrock	58	P14
Cross Av., D.L.	60	U16
Cross Guns Bri. 7	35	J6
Cross Kevin St. 8	43	K10
Crosthwaite Pk. E.,	61	V17
D.L.		
Crosthwaite Pk. S.,	61	V17
D.L.		
Crosthwaite Pk. W.,	61	V17
D.L.		
Crosthwaite Ter.,	61	V16
D.L.		
Crotty Av. 12	47	E12
Crow St. 2	43	K9
Crown All. 2	43	K9
Temple Bar		
Croydon Gdns. 3	36	M5
Croydon Grn. 3	36	M6
Croydon Pk. Av. 3	36	M5
Croydon Ter. 3	36	M5
Crumlin Pk. 12	47	F11
Crumlin Rd. 12	47	F11
Cuala Rd. 7	34	H6
Cuckoo La. 7	43	J8
Cuffe La. 2	43	K10
Cuffe St. 2	43	K10
Cullenswood Gdns. 6	50	L12
Cullenswood Pk. 6	50	L12
Cumberland St. 2	44	L10
Cumberland St., D.L.	60	U16

Cumberland St. N. 1	35	K7
Cumberland St. S. 2	44	L9
Curlew Rd. 12	47	E11
Curved St. 2	43	K9
Eustace St.		
Curzon St. 8	43	K10
Custom Ho. 1	44	L8
Custom Ho. Quay 1	44	L8
Cymric Rd. 4	45	O9
Cypress Downs 6	53	F15
Cypress Dr. 6	53	F15
Cypress Garth 6	53	F15
Cypress Gro. N. 6	53	F15
Cypress Gro. Rd. 6	53	F15
Cypress Gro. S. 6	53	F15
Cypress Lawn 6	53	F15
Cypress Pk. 6	53	F15
Cypress Rd.,	57	O15
Stillorgan		

D

Dalcassian Downs 11	35	J6
Dale Clo., Stillorgan	57	O16
Dale Dr., Stillorgan	57	O16
Dame Ct. 2	43	K9
Dame St. 2	43	K9
Danes Ct. 3	39	R6
Danesfort 3	38	P6
Daneswell Rd. 9	35	K5
Dangan Av. 12	47	F13
Dangan Dr. 12	47	F13
Dangan Pk. 12	47	F13
Daniel St. 8	43	J10
Danieli Dr. 5	26	P4
Danieli Rd. 5	26	P4
Dargle Rd. 9	35	K6
Darley St. 6	49	J11
Darleys Ter. 8	42	H10
Darling Est. 7	33	E5
Thomas Davis St. S.		
Davitt Rd. 12	41	E10
Dawson Ct. 2	43	K9
Stephen St.		
Dawson Ct., D.L.	58	Q15
Dawson La. 2	44	L9
Dawson St. 2	43	K9
De Burgh Rd. 7	42	G8
De Courcy Sq. 9	35	J5
De Vesci Ter., D.L.	60	U16
Dean St. 8	43	J9
Dean Swift Grn. 11	23	K3
Dean Swift Rd. 11	23	J3
Dean Swift Sq. 8	43	J9
Swifts All.		
Deans Gra. Cem., D.L.	60	S17
Deans Gra. Rd.,	59	S16
Stillorgan		
Deanstown Av. 11	21	F3
Deanstown Dr. 11	21	F3
Deanstown Grn. 11	21	F3
Deanstown Pk. 11	21	F3
Deanstown Rd. 11	21	F3
Decies Rd. 10	40	C9
Deerpark Av.,	32	C5
Castleknock		
Deerpark Clo.,	32	C5
Castleknock		
Deerpark Dr.,	32	C5
Castleknock		
Deerpark Lawn,	32	C5
Castleknock		
Deerpark Rd.,	32	C5
Castleknock		
Deerpark Rd.,	57	O15
Stillorgan		

Del Val Av.,	28	U3
Kilbarrack		
Del Val Ct.,	28	U3
Kilbarrack		
Delville Rd. 11	23	J3
Delvin Rd. 7	34	H6
Demesne 5	38	P5
Denmark St. Great 1	35	K7
Denzille La. 2	44	L9
Denzille Pl. 2	44	L9
Denzille La.		
Department of	42	G8
Defence 7		
Infirmary Rd.		
Department of	35	K5
Defence 9		
St. Mobhi Rd.		
Dermot O'Hurley Av. 4	45	N9
Derravaragh Rd. 6	48	G13
Derry Dr. 12	47	F12
Derry Pk. 12	47	F12
Derry Rd. 12	47	F12
Derrynane Gdns. 4	45	N10
Derrynane Par. 7	35	K7
Desmond Av., D.L.	61	U16
Desmond St. 8	43	J10
Devenish Rd. 12	48	G12
Deverell Pl. 1	44	L8
Deverys La. 7	35	J6
Devoy Rd. 8	41	F10
Diamond 1	36	L7
Digges La. 2	43	K9
Stephen St.		
Digges St. 2	43	K10
Digges St. Lwr. 2	43	K10
Cuffe La.		
Dingle Rd. 7	34	G6
Dispensary La. 14	55	J16
Distillery Rd. 3	36	L6
Dock Pl. S. 4	44	M9
Dock St. S.		
Dock St. S. 4	44	M9
Dodder Dale 14	54	H15
Dodder Grd. 14	50	L13
Dodder Pk. Dr. 14	55	J14
Dodder Pk. Gro. 14	55	J14
Dodder Pk. Rd. 14	55	J14
Dodder Ter. 4	45	N9
Doddervale 6	55	K14
D'Olier St. 2	43	K8
Dollymount Av. 3	39	R6
Dollymount Gro. 3	39	R6
Dollymount Pk. 3	39	R6
Dollymount Ri. 3	39	R6
Dolphin Av. 8	42	H10
Dolphin Mkt. 8	42	H10
Dolphin's Barn St.		
Dolphin Rd. 12	42	G10
Dolphin's Barn 8	42	H10
Dolphin's Barn St. 8	42	H10
Dominican Convent 7	33	F5
Dominick La. 1	43	K8
Dominick Pl. 1	43	K8
Dominick St., D.L.	61	U16
Dominick St. Lwr. 1	43	K8
Dominick St. Upper 7	35	J7
Domville Dr. 12	53	F15
Domville Rd. 12	53	F15
Donaghmede Av. 5	28	T2
Donaghmede Dr. 5	28	T2
Donaghmede Pk. 5	28	T2
Donaghmede Rd. 5	27	S2
Donard Rd. 12	47	E11
Donelan Av. 8	42	G9
Donnybrook Castle	51	N13
Ct. 4		
Donnybrook Clo. 4	51	N12
Donnybrook Grn. 4	51	N12
Donnybrook Manor 4	50	M12
Donnybrook Rd. 4	50	M12
Donnycarney Rd. 9	37	N5
Donnycastle 4	51	N12
Donore Av. 8	42	H10
Donore Rd. 8	42	H10
Donore Ter. 8	42	H10
Brown St. S.		
Donovans La. 8	43	J10
Clanbrassil St. Lwr.		
Doon Av. 7	34	H7
Doris St. 4	45	N9

Dornden Pk., Booterstown	63	P13
Dorset La. 1	35	K7
Dorset Pl. 1	35	K7
Dorset St. Lwr.		
Dorset St. Lwr. 1	35	K7
Dorset St. Upper 1	35	K7
Dowkers La. 8	43	J10
Dowland Rd. 12	47	E12
Dowling's Ct. 2	44	L9
Lombard St. E.		
Dowling's Ct. S. 2	44	L9
Lombard St. E.		
Downpatrick Rd. 12	48	G11
Dowth Av. 7	34	H6
Drapier Grn. 11	23	J3
Drapier Rd. 11	23	J3
Drayton Clo., D.L.	60	T16
Drimnagh Castle 12	46	D11
Drimnagh Rd. 12	47	E11
Dromard Rd. 12	47	E11
Dromawling Rd. 9	25	N3
Dromdawn Av. 9	25	N3
Dromeen Av. 9	25	N3
Dromlee Cres. 9	25	N3
Dromnanane Pk. 9	25	N3
Dromnanane Rd. 9	25	N3
Dromore Rd. 12	47	F11
Drumalee Av. 7	34	H7
Drumalee Rd.		
Drumalee Ct. 7	34	H7
Drumalee Rd.		
Drumalee Dr. 7	34	H7
Drumalee Rd.		
Drumalee Gro. 7	34	H7
Drumalee Rd.		
Drumalee Pk. 7	34	H7
Drumalee Rd. 7	34	H7
Drumcliffe Dr. 7	34	G6
Drumcliffe Rd. 7	34	G6
Drumcondra Hosp. 3	35	K6
Drumcondra Pk. 3	36	L6
Drumcondra Rd. Lwr. 9	35	K6
Drumcondra Rd. Upper 9	36	L5
Drummartin Clo. 14	57	N16
Drummartin Cres. 14	57	N16
Drummartin Rd. 14	57	N16
Drummartin Ter. 14	57	N16
Drummond Pl. 6	49	J11
Mount Drummond Av.		
Druncondra Bri. 9	36	L5
Drury St. 2	43	K9
Dublin City University 9	23	K3
Dublin Corporation Food Mkt. 7	43	J8
St. Michan's St.		
Dublin Rd., Howth	30	X2
Dublin Rd., Kilbarrack	29	V3
Dublin Rd., Stillorgan	58	P16
Dublin St., Baldoyle	29	V2
Dufferin Av. 8	43	J10
Duggan Pl. 6	49	K12
Rathmines Rd. Upper		
Duke La. 2	43	K9
Duke La. Lwr. 2	43	K9
Duke St.		
Duke Row 1	36	L7
North Circular Rd.		
Duke St. 2	43	K9
Dún Laoghaire Sta., D.L.	61	V16
Dunamase, D.L.	58	Q15
Dunard Av. 7	34	G6
Dunard Ct. 7	34	G7
Dunard Dr. 7	34	G7
Dunard Pk. 7	34	G7
Dunard Rd. 7	34	G7
Dunard Wk. 7	34	G7
Dunbo Ter., Howth	31	AA2
Church St.		
Duncarrig, Howth	30	Y3
Dundaniel Rd. 5	25	N2
Dundela Av., D.L.	61	W17
Dundela Haven, D.L.	61	W17
Dundrum Rd. 14	56	L16
Dunedin Clo., D.L.	60	T17
Dunedin Ct., D.L.	60	T17

Dunedin Dr., D.L.	60	T17
Dunedin Pk., D.L.	60	T17
Dunedin Ter., D.L.	60	T17
Dungar Ter., D.L.	61	V16
Northumberland Av.		
Dungriffan Rd., Howth	31	BB3
Dunleary Hill, D.L.	60	U16
Dunleary Rd., D.L.	60	U15
Dunluce Rd. 3	38	P5
Dunmanus Rd. 7	34	G6
Dunne St. 1	36	L7
Dunree Pk. 5	26	Q2
Dunseverick Rd. 3	38	P5
Dunsink Av. 11	21	F3
Dunsink Dr. 11	21	F3
Dunsink Gdns. 11	22	G3
Dunsink Grn. 11	22	G3
Dunsink La., Castleknock	20	C3
Dunsink Observatory, Castleknock	20	D3
Dunsink Pk. 11	21	F3
Dunsink Rd. 11	22	G3
Dunville Av. 6	50	L12
Dunville Ter. 6	49	K11
Mountpleasant Av. Upper		
Durham Rd. 4	51	O11
Durrow Rd. 12	48	G12

E

Eagle Hill, D.L.	59	R15
Eagle Hill Av. 6	48	H13
Earl Pl. 1	43	K8
Earl St. N. 1	43	K8
Earl St. S. 8	43	J9
Earls Ct. 7	34	G7
Earlsfort Mans. 2	43	K10
Adelaide Rd.		
Earlsfort Ter. 2	43	K10
East Oil Jetty 1	62	P9
East Rd. 3	44	M8
East Wall Rd. 3	36	M7
Eastern Breakwater 1	62	P9
Eastmoreland La. 4	44	M10
Eastmoreland Pl. 4	44	M10
Eastwood Clo. 11	21	F3
Eastwood Cres. 11	21	E3
Eastwood Pk. 11	21	F3
Eaton Brae 14	55	K14
Eaton Pl., D.L.	59	S15
Eaton Rd. 6	48	H13
Eaton Sq. 6	48	H13
Eaton Sq., D.L.	59	S15
Ebenezer Ter. 8	42	H10
Eblana Av., D.L.	61	V16
Eblana Vills. 2	44	M9
Grand Canal St. Lwr.		
Eccles Ct. 7	35	K7
Eccles Pl.		
Eccles Pl. 7	35	K7
Eccles St. 7	35	K7
Echlin St. 8	42	H9
Eden Pk., D.L.	61	V17
Eden Pk. Dr. 14	57	N16
Eden Pk. Rd. 14	57	N16
Eden Quay 1	43	K8
Eden Rd. Lwr., D.L.	61	V17
Eden Rd. Upper, D.L.	61	V17
Eden Ter., D.L.	61	V17
Eden Vills., D.L.	61	V17
Edenbrook Ct. 14	54	H16
Edenbrook Dr. 14	54	G16
Edenbrook Pk. 14	54	G16
Edenmore Av. 5	26	Q3
Edenmore Cres. 5	27	R3
Edenmore Dr. 5	27	R3
Edenmore Gdns. 5	27	R3
Edenmore Grn. 5	27	R3
Edenmore Gro. 5	26	Q3
Edenvale Rd. 6	50	L12
Effra Rd. 6	49	J12
Eglinton Ct. 4	50	M12
Eglinton Pk. 4	50	M12
Eglinton Pk., D.L.	60	U16
Eglinton Rd. 4	50	M12
Eglinton Sq. 4	50	M12
Eglinton Ter. 4	50	M12
Eglinton Ter. 14	56	M16

Eldon Ter. 8	43	J10
South Circular Rd.		
Elgin Rd. 4	50	M11
Elizabeth St. 3	36	L6
Elkwood 14	54	G16
Ellenfield Rd. 9	24	M3
Ellesmere Av. 7	34	H7
Ellis Quay 7	42	H8
Elliss St. 7	42	H8
Benburb St.		
Elm Gro., D.L.	59	R16
Elm Gro. Cotts. 7	33	E6
Blackhorse Av.		
Elm Mt. Av. 9	25	N4
Elm Mt. Clo. 9	25	N4
Elm Mt. Ct. 9	25	O4
Elm Mt. Cres. 5	25	N3
Elm Mt. Dr. 9	25	N4
Elm Mt. Gro. 9	25	N3
Elm Mt. Hts. 9	25	N3
Elm Mt. Lawn 9	25	N3
Elm Mt. Pk. 9	25	N3
Elm Mt. Ri. 9	25	N4
Elm Mt. Rd. 5	25	N4
Elm Mt. Rd. 9	25	N4
Elm Mt. Vw. 9	25	N4
Elm Pk. 4	51	O13
Elm Rd. 9	25	N4
Elmpark Av. 6	50	L12
Elmpark Ter. 6	48	H13
Elms, The 4	51	O13
Elms, The, D.L.	58	Q15
Elmwood Av. Lwr. 6	50	L11
Elmwood Av. Upper		
Elmwood Av. Upper 6	50	L11
Elton Ct. 5	27	R2
Elton Dr.		
Elton Dr. 5	27	R2
Elton Pk. 5	27	R2
Elton Pk., D.L.	61	W17
Elton Wk. 5	27	R2
Elton Dr.		
Ely Pl. 2	44	L10
Ely Pl. Upper 2	44	L10
Ely Pl.		
Embassy Lawn 14	56	M14
Emerald Cotts. 4	44	M10
Emerald Pl. 1	44	M8
Sheriff St. Lwr.		
Emerald Sq. 8	42	H10
Emerald St. 1	44	M8
Emily Pl. 1	44	L8
Sheriff St. Lwr.		
Emmet Ct. 8	41	E10
Emmet Rd. 8	41	F9
Emmet Sq., D.L.	58	Q14
Emmet St. 1	36	L7
Emmet St. (Haroldscross) 6	49	J11
Emor St. 8	43	J10
Emorville Av. 8	43	J10
Emorville Sq. 8	43	J10
South Circular Rd.		
Empress Pl. 1	36	L7
Enaville Rd. 3	36	M7
Engine All. 8	43	J9
Ennafort Av.	26	Q4
(Ascal Dun Eanna) 5		
Ennafort Ct. 5	26	Q4
Ennafort Dr.	26	Q4
(Ceide Dun Eanna) 5		
Ennafort Gro. 5	26	Q4
Ennafort Pk. 5	26	Q4
Ennafort Rd. 5	26	Q4
Ennel Av. 5	26	Q3
Ennel Dr. 5	26	Q3
Ennel Pk. 5	26	Q3
Ennel Rd.	26	Q3
(Bothar Ainninn) 5		
Ennis Gro. 4	45	N10
Enniskerry Rd. 7	35	J6
Erne Pl. 2	44	M9
Erne Pl. Little 2	44	M9
Erne St. Lwr. 2	44	M9
Erne St. Upper 2	44	M9
Erne Ter. Front 2	44	M9
Erne St. Upper		
Erne Ter. Rere 2	44	M9
Erne St. Upper		
Errigal Gdns. 12	47	E11

Errigal Rd. 12	47	E11
Erris Rd. 7	34	H6
Esmond Av. 3	36	M6
Esposito Rd. 12	47	E12
Essex Quay 8	43	K9
Essex St. E. 2	43	K9
Essex St. W. 8	43	K9
Estate Av. 4	63	P13
Estate Cotts. 4	44	M10
Northumberland Rd.		
Eugene St. 8	42	H10
Eustace St. 2	43	K9
Everton Av. 7	34	H7
Evora Pk., Howth	31	AA3
Evora Ter., Howth	31	AA2
St. Lawrence Rd.		
Ewington La. 8	42	H9
Exchange Ct. 2	43	K9
Dame St.		
Exchange St. Lwr. 8	43	K9
Exchange St. Upper 8	43	K9
Lord Edward St.		
Exchequer St. 2	43	K9

F

Faber Ct., D.L.	60	T17
Fade St. 2	43	K9
Fairbrook Lawn 14	54	H16
Fairfield Av. 3	36	M7
Fairfield Pk. 6	49	J13
Fairfield Rd. (Glasnevin) 9	35	K5
Fairlawn Pk. 11	22	G4
Fairlawn Rd.		
Fairlawn Rd. 11	22	G4
Fairview 3	36	M6
Fairview Av. (Irishtown) 4	45	N9
Fairview Av. Lwr. 3	36	M6
Fairview Av. Upper 3	36	M6
Fairview Grn. 3	36	M6
Fairview Pas. 3	36	M6
Fairview Strand		
Fairview Strand 3	36	M6
Fairview Ter. 3	36	M6
Fairways 14	54	G15
Fairways Av. 11	22	H3
Fairways Grn. 11	22	H3
Fairways Pk. 11	22	H3
Faith Av. 3	36	M7
Falcarragh Rd. 9	24	L3
Farmhill Dr. 14	56	M15
Farmhill Pk. 14	57	N16
Farmhill Rd. 14	56	M15
Farney Pk. 4	45	O10
Farnham Cres. 11	22	G3
Farnham Dr. 11	22	G3
Farrenboley Cotts. 14	56	L14
Farrenboley Pk. 14	56	L14
Father Matthew Bri. 8	43	J9
Fatima Mans. 8	42	G10
Faughart Rd. 12	48	G12
Faussagh Av. 7	34	G6
Faussagh Rd. 7	34	H6
Fenian St. 2	44	L9
Fergus Rd. 6	54	H14
Ferguson Rd. 9	35	K5
Ferndale Av. 11	22	H3
Ferndale Rd. 11	22	H3
Fernhill Av. 12	53	E14
Fernhill Pk. 12	53	E14
Fernhill Rd. 12	53	E14
Ferns Rd. 12	48	G12
Fernvale Dr. 12	47	F11
Ferrard Rd. 6	49	J13
Ferrymans Crossing 1	44	M8
Fertullagh Rd. 7	34	H6
Field Av. 12	47	E12
Fields Ter. 6	50	L11
Ranelagh Rd.		
Fifth Av. 8	42	G10
Findlater Pl. 1	43	K8
Parnell St.		
Findlater St., D.L.	61	V17
Findlaters St. 7	42	G8
Fingal Av. (Clontarf) 3	38	Q6
Fingal Pl. 7	34	H7
Fingal St. 8	42	H10
Finglas Pk. 11	22	H2

Name	Page	Grid
Finglas Pl. 11	22	G3
Finglas Rd. 11	34	H5
Finglas Rd. Old 11	23	J4
Finlay Sq., Stillorgan	57	O15
Finn St. 7	42	H8
Finsbury Pk. 14	56	L16
Firhouse Rd. 14	53	E16
First Av. 1	44	M8
First Av. (Inchicore) 10	40	D9
Fishamble St. 8	43	J9
Fitzgerald Pk., D.L.	60	U17
Fitzgerald St. 6	49	J11
Fitzgibbon La. 1	36	L7
Fitzgibbon St. 1	36	L7
Fitzmaurice Rd. 11	23	J3
Fitzroy Av. 3	36	L6
Fitzwilliam Ct. 2	44	L10
Pembroke St. Upper		
Fitzwilliam La. 2	44	L10
Fitzwilliam Pl. 2	44	L10
Fitzwilliam Quay 4	45	N9
Fitzwilliam Sq. E. 2	44	L10
Fitzwilliam Sq. N. 2	44	L10
Fitzwilliam Sq. S. 2	44	L10
Fitzwilliam Sq. W. 2	44	L10
Fitzwilliam St. (Ringsend) 4		
Fitzwilliam St. Lwr. 2	44	L10
Fitzwilliam St. Upper 2	44	L10
Fleet St. 2	43	K9
Fleming Rd. 9	35	K5
Flemings La. 4	44	M10
Haddington Rd.		
Flemings Pl. 4	44	L10
Flemingstown Pk. 14	56	L15
Fleurville, D.L.	59	R16
Floraville, D.L. (Donnybrook) 4	50	M12
Florence St. 8	49	K11
Lennox St.		
Foley St. 1	44	L8
Fontenoy St. 7	35	J7
Fonthill Pk. 14	54	H16
Fonthill Rd. 14	54	H16
Forbes La. 8	42	H9
Forbes St. 2	44	M9
Fortfield Av. 6	54	G14
Fortfield Ct. 6	54	G14
Fortfield Dr. 6	54	G14
Fortfield Gdns. 6	49	K13
Fortfield Gro. 6	54	G14
Fortfield Pk. 6	54	G15
Fortfield Ter. 6	49	K13
Forth Rd. 3	37	N7
Fortview Av. 3	38	Q7
Foster Cotts. 7	35	J7
Phibsborough Rd.		
Foster Pl. S. 2	43	K9
Foster Ter. 3	36	L7
Fosterbrook, D.L.	58	P14
Fosters, The, Stillorgan	57	O15
Fosters Av., Stillorgan	57	O15
Fountain Pl. 7	43	J8
Fountain Rd. 8	42	G8
Fourth Av. 1	44	M8
Fourth Av. 8	42	G10
Fownes St. 2	43	K9
Foxfield Av. 5	27	S3
Foxfield Cres. 5	28	T3
Foxfield Dr. 5	28	T3
Foxfield Grn. 5	28	T3
Foxfield Gro. 5	27	S3
Foxfield Hts. 5	28	T3
Foxfield Lawn 5	28	T3
Foxfield Pk. 5	28	T4
Foxfield Rd. 5	27	S3
Foxfield St. John 5	28	T3
Foxhill Av. 5	27	R2
Foxhill Clo. 5	27	R2
Foxhill Ct. 5	27	R2
Foxhill Cres. 5	27	R2
Foxhill Dr. 5	27	R2
Foxhill Grn. 5	27	R2
Foxhill Gro. 5	27	R2
Foxhill Lawn 5	27	R2
Foxhill Pk. 5	27	R2
Foxhill Way 5	27	R2
Foxs La. 5	28	T4
Foyle Rd. 3	36	M6
Francis St. 8	43	J9
Frankfort 14	56	L15
Frankfort Av. 6	49	K13
Frankfort Ct. 6	49	J13
Frankfort Pk. 14	56	L15
Frascati Pk., D.L.	59	R15
Frascati Rd., D.L.	59	R15
Frederick St. 1	35	K7
Hardwicke St.		
Frederick La. 2	44	L9
Frederick La. N. 1	35	K7
Frederick St. N. 1	35	K7
Frederick St. S. 2	44	L9
Frenchmans La. 1	44	L8
Gardiner St. Lwr.		
Friarsland Av. 14	56	M15
Friarsland Rd. 14	56	M15
Friary Av. 7	43	J8
Fumballys La. 8	43	J10
Furry Pk. 5	38	P5
Furry Pk. Ct. 5	38	P5
Furry Pk. Rd. 5	38	Q5
Furze Rd., Castleknock	32	C7

G

Name	Page	Grid
Gaelic St. 3	36	M7
Gairdini Sheinleasa 9	23	K2
Galmoy Rd. 7	34	H6
Galtymore Clo. 12	41	E10
Galtymore Dr. 12	41	F10
Galtymore Pk. 12	47	E11
Galtymore Rd. 12	47	E11
Gandon Clo. 8	49	J11
Garden Croath, Stillorgan	59	R16
Garden La. 8	43	J9
Gardiner La. 1	36	L7
Gardiner Row 1	35	K7
Gardiner St. Lwr. 1	36	L7
Gardiner St. Middle 1	36	L7
Gardiner St. Upper 1	35	K7
Gardiner's Pl. 1	35	K7
Gardini Lein (Lein Gdns.) 5	26	Q4
Gardini Phairc An Bhailtini (Villa Pk. Gdns.)	23	F6
Garriglea Gdns., D.L.	60	U17
Garryowen Rd. 10	40	C9
Gartan Av. 9	35	K6
Garville Av. 6	49	J13
Garville Av. Upper 6	49	J13
Garville Rd. 6	49	J13
Geoffrey Keating Rd. 8	43	J10
O'Curry Rd.		
George's Av., D.L.	59	R15
George's Hill 7	43	J8
George's La. 7	43	J8
George's Pl. 1	35	K7
George's Pl., Blackrock	59	R15
George's Pl., D.L.	61	U16
George's Quay 2	44	L8
George's St. Lwr., D.L.	60	U16
George's St. Upper, D.L.	61	V16
Gerald St. 4	44	M9
Geraldine St. 7	35	J7
Geraldine Ter. 6	50	L13
Gilbert Rd. 8	43	J10
Gilford Av. 4	51	O11
Gilford Ct. 4	51	O11
Gilford Dr. 4	51	O11
Gilford Pk. 4	51	O11
Gilford Rd. 4	51	O11
Glandore Pk., D.L.	60	U17
Glandore Rd. 9	36	M5
Glasanaon Ct. 11	22	H3
Glasanaon Pk.		
Glasanaon Pk. 11	22	H3
Glasanaon Rd. 11	22	H3
Glasaree Rd. 11	22	H3
Glasgow Ct. 14	56	L14
Glasilawn Av. 11	23	J4
Glasilawn Rd. 11	22	H4
Glasmeen Rd. 11	22	H4
Glasnamana Pl. 11	23	J4
Glasnamana Rd. 11	22	H4
Glasnevin Av. 11	22	H2
Glasnevin Bri. 9	35	K5
Glasnevin Ct. 11	22	H4
Glasnevin Downs 11	22	H4
Glasnevin Dr. 11	23	J3
Glasnevin Hill 9	35	K5
Glasnevin Rd. 11	22	H4
Glasnevin Wds. 11	22	H4
Glasthule Bldgs., D.L.	61	W17
Glasthule Rd., D.L.	61	W17
Gleann Na Smol, 12	59	S16
Glebe Vw. 11	22	G3
Gledswood Av. 14	56	M14
Gledswood Clo. 14	56	M14
Gledswood Dr. 14	56	M14
Gledswood Pk. 14	56	M14
Glen, The, D.L.	61	V17
Glengara Clo.		
Glenaan Rd. 9	24	L3
Glenabbey Rd., Stillorgan	57	O16
Glenageary Rd. Lwr., D.L.	61	V17
Glenageary Rd. Upper, D.L.	60	U17
Glenageary Wds., D.L.	61	U17
Glenanne 12	48	G13
Glenard Av. 7	34	H7
Glenarm Av. 9	36	L6
Glenarm Sq. 9	36	L6
Glenarriff Rd., Ashtown	33	E5
Glenart Av., D.L.	58	O16
Glenaulin Dr. (Ceide Glennaluinn), Chapelizod	40	C8
Glenavy Pk. 6	48	G13
Glenayle Rd. 5	27	R2
Glenayr Rd. 6	55	J14
Glenbeigh Pk. 7	34	G7
Glenbeigh Rd. 7	34	G7
Glenbower Pk. 14	56	L16
Glenbrook Pk. 14	54	H16
Glenbrook Rd. 7	33	E5
Glencar Rd. 7	34	G7
Glencarrig, Howth	30	Y2
Glencloy Rd. 9	24	L3
Glencorp Rd. 9	24	M3
Glendale Pk. 12	53	F14
Glendalough Rd. 9	35	K6
Glendhu Pk., Ashtown	33	E5
Glendhu Rd., Ashtown	33	E5
Glendoo Clo. 12	52	C14
Lugnaquilla Av.		
Glendown Av. 12	53	E14
Glendown Clo. 12	53	E14
Glendown Gro.		
Glendown Ct. 12	53	E14
Glendown Cres. 12	53	E14
Glendown Grn. 12	53	E14
Glendown Gro.		
Glendown Gro. 12	53	E14
Glendown Lawn 12	53	F14
Glendown Pk. 12	53	F14
Glendown Rd. 12	53	F14
Glendun Rd. 9	24	L3
Glenealy Rd. 12	48	H11
Glenfarne Rd. 5	26	Q2
Glengara Clo., D.L.	61	V17
Glengara Pk., D.L.	61	V17
Glengariff Par. 7	35	K6
Glenhill Av. 11	22	H3
Glenhill Ct. 11	22	H3
Glenhill Dr. 11	22	H3
Glenhill Gro. 11	22	H3
Glenhill Rd. 11	22	H3
Glenhill Vills. 11	22	H3
Glenhill Pk.		
Glenmalure Pk. 8	42	G10
Glenmalure Sq. 6	50	L13
Glenmore Rd. 7	34	G7
Glenomena Gro., Booterstown	57	O14
Glenomena Pk., Booterstown	51	O13
Glenshesk Rd. 9	24	M3
Glenties Dr. 11	21	F4
Glenties Pk. 11	21	F4
Glentow Rd. 9	24	L3
Glentworth Pk. 5	27	R2
Slademore Av.		
Glenvar Pk., D.L.	58	Q15
Glenview Lawns, Tallaght	52	D16
Glenview Pk., Tallaght	52	C16
Glenwood Rd. 5	26	Q3
Gloucester La. 1	44	L8
Sean McDermott St. Lwr.		
Gloucester Pl. 1	36	L7
Gloucester Pl. Lwr. 1	44	L8
Gloucester Pl. Upper 1	36	L7
Gloucester St. S. 2	44	L8
Gloucester Ter. 1	36	L7
Glovers All. 2	43	K9
Goatstown Av. 14	56	M15
Goatstown Rd. 14	57	N15
Golden Bri. 8	41	E9
Golden La. 8	43	K9
Goldenbridge Av. 8	41	F10
Goldenbridge Gdns. 8	41	F10
Goldenbridge Ter. 8	41	F9
Connolly Av.		
Goldsmith St. 7	35	J7
Gordon Pl. 2	43	K10
Richmond St. S.		
Gordon St. 4	44	M9
Gorsefield Ct. 5	26	Q3
Gortbeg Av. 11	22	G4
Gortbeg Rd.		
Gortbeg Dr. 11	22	G4
Gortbeg Rd.		
Gortbeg Pk. 11	22	G4
Gortbeg Rd.		
Gortbeg Rd. 11	22	G4
Gortmore Av. 11	22	G4
Gortmore Dr. 11	22	G4
Gortmore Pk. 11	22	G4
Gortmore Rd.		
Gortmore Rd. 11	22	G4
Government Building 2	44	L9
Grace O'Malley Dr., Howth	31	AA3
Grace O'Malley Rd., Howth	31	AA3
Grace Pk. Av. 3	36	L6
Grace Pk. Ct. 9	24	M3
Grace Pk. Gdns. 9	36	L5
Grace Pk. Hts. 9	24	M4
Grace Pk. Meadows 9	25	N4
Grace Pk. Rd. 9	36	L5
Grace Pk. Ter. 9	36	M5
Gracefield Av. 5	26	Q4
Gracefield Ct. 5	26	P4
Gracefield Rd. 5	26	P4
Grafton St. 2	43	K9
Graham St. 1	35	K7
Granby La. 1	35	K7
Granby Pl. 1	43	K8
Granby Row 1	35	K7
Grand Canal Bk. (Ranelagh) 6	49	K11
Grand Canal Bk. 8	42	H10
Grand Canal Harbour 8	42	H9
James's St.		
Grand Canal Pl. N. 8	42	H9
Grand Canal Quay 2	44	M9
Grand Canal St. Lwr. 2	44	M9
Grand Canal St. Upper 4	44	M10
Grand Canal Vw. 8	42	G10
Grand Par. 6	49	K11
Grange Av., Baldoyle	28	U2
Grange Clo., Baldoyle	28	U2
Grange Downs 14	55	J16
Grange Dr., Baldoyle	28	U2
Grange Gro., D.L.	60	S17
Grange Par., Baldoyle	28	U2
Grange Pk. 14	54	H16
Grange Pk. Av. 5	27	S3
Grange Pk. Clo. 5	27	S3
Grange Pk. Cres. 5	27	S3
Grange Pk. Dr. 5	27	S3
Grange Pk. Grn. 5	27	S3
Grange Pk. Gro. 5	27	S3

Name	Page	Grid
Grange Pk. Par. 5	27	S3
Grange Pk. Ri. 5	27	S3
Grange Pk. Rd. 5	27	S3
Grange Pk. Wk. 5	27	S3
Grange Ri., Baldoyle	28	U2
Grange Rd. 5	27	S2
Grange Rd. 14	54	H16
Grange Way, Baldoyle	28	U2
Grangegorman Lwr. 7	43	J8
Grangegorman Upper 7	35	J7
Grangemore Av. 5	27	S2
Grangemore Ct. 5	27	S2
Rosapenna Dr.		
Grangemore Gro. 5	27	S2
Grangemore Pk. 5	27	S2
Rosapenna Dr.		
Grangemore Ri. 5	27	S2
Rosapenna Dr.		
Granite Hall, D.L.	61	V17
Granite Pl. 4	51	N11
Granite Ter. 8	41	E9
Inchicore Ter. S.		
Grantham Pl. 8	43	K10
Grantham St. 8	43	K10
Grants Row 2	44	M9
Grattan Ct. E. 2	44	M9
Grattan St.		
Grattan Cres. 8	41	E9
Grattan Par. 9	35	K6
Grattan Pl. 2	44	M9
Grattan St.		
Grattan St. 2	44	M9
Gray Sq. 8	43	J9
Pimlico		
Gray St. 8	43	J9
Graysbrook, Howth	31	BB3
Great Clarence Pl. 2	44	M9
Great Western Av. 7	35	J7
North Circular Rd.		
Great Western Sq. 7	35	J7
Great Western Vills. 7	35	J7
Greek St. 7	43	J8
Green Pk. 14	55	K14
Green Rd., D.L.	58	Q15
Green St. 7	43	J8
Green St. E. 2	45	N9
Green St. Little 7	43	J8
Greenacre Ct. 14	53	E16
Greenacre Av. 5	26	P2
Greencastle Cres. 5	26	P2
Greencastle Dr. 5	26	P2
Greencastle Par. 5	26	Q2
Greendale Av. 5	28	T3
Greendale Rd. 5	28	T3
Greenfield Cres. 4	51	N13
Greenfield Pk. 4	51	N13
Greenfield Rd., Howth	30	X2
Greenfield Rd., Stillorgan	58	P15
Greenhills Rd., Tallaght	52	C15
Greenlands, The 14	55	J15
Greenlea Av. 6	54	G14
Greenlea Dr. 6	54	G14
Greenlea Gro. 6	54	G14
Greenlea Pk. 6	54	G14
Greenlea Rd. 6	54	G14
Greenmount Av. 12	49	J11
Greenmount Ct. 12	49	J11
Greenmount Av.		
Greenmount La. 12	49	J11
Greenmount Lawns 6	54	H14
Greenmount Rd. 6	49	J13
Greenmount Sq. 12	49	J11
Greenmount Av.		
Greenore Ter. 2	44	M9
Grattan St.		
Greentrees Dr. 12	53	E14
Greentrees Pk. 12	47	E13
Greentrees Rd. 12	53	E14
Greenville Av. 8	43	J10
Greenville Rd., D.L.	59	S16
Greenville Ter. 8	43	J10
Greenwich Ct. 6	49	K12
Greenwood Av. 5	27	R2
Grenville La. 1	35	K7
Grenville St. 1	35	K7
Greygates, D.L.	58	P15
Greyhound Race Track 6	49	J12
Greys La., Howth	31	BB4
Griffith Av. 9	23	K4
Griffith Av. 11	23	J4
Griffith Clo. 11	22	H4
Griffith Ct. 9	36	M5
Griffith Downs 9	24	L4
Griffith Dr. 11	22	H3
Griffith Lawns 9	23	K4
Griffith Par. 11	22	H4
Griffith Rd. 11	22	H4
Griffith Sq. 8	49	J11
Wesley Pl.		
Griffith Sq. S. 8	43	J10
South Circular Rd.		
Griffith Wk. 9	36	M5
Grosvenor Ct. 3	38	P5
Grosvenor Ct. 12	53	F14
Grosvenor Lo. 6	49	J12
Grosvenor Pk. 6	49	J12
Grosvenor Pl. 6	49	J12
Grosvenor Rd. 6	49	J12
Grosvenor Sq. 6	49	J12
Grosvenor Ter., D.L.	60	U16
Grosvenor Vills. 6	49	J12
Grotto Av., Booterstown	58	P14
Grotto Pl., Booterstown	58	P14
Grove, The 5	27	S4
Grove, The 9	24	M4
Grove Av. 6	49	J11
Grove Rd.		
Grove Av., Blackrock	58	Q15
Grove Ho. Gdns., Stillorgan	58	Q16
Grove Lawn, Stillorgan	58	Q15
Grove Pk. 6	49	K11
Grove Pk. Av. 11	22	H2
Grove Pk. Cres. 11	23	J2
Grove Pk. Dr. 11	22	H2
Grove Pk. Rd. 11	22	H2
Grove Rd. (Rathmines) 6	49	J11
Grove Rd. (Finglas) 11	22	H2
Grove Wd. 11	22	H2
Guild St. 1	44	M8
Guinness Brewery 8	42	H9
Gulistan Cotts. 6	49	K11
Gulistan Pl. 6	49	K12
Gulistan Ter. 6	49	K11

H

Name	Page	Grid
H.S. Reilly Bri. 11	33	F5
Haddington Rd. 4	44	M10
Haddington Rd. 4	44	M10
Haddington Ter., D.L.	61	V16
Haddon Pk. 3	37	O6
Seaview Av. N.		
Haddon Rd. 3	37	O6
Hagans Ct. 2	44	L10
Haigh Ter., D.L.	61	V16
Halliday Rd. 7	42	H8
Halliday Sq. 7	42	H8
Halston St. 7	43	J8
Hamilton St. 8	42	H10
Hammond La. 7	43	J8
Hammond St. 8	43	J10
Hampstead Av. 9	23	K4
Hampstead Ct. 9	23	K3
Hampstead Pk. 9	23	K4
Hampton Convent 9	36	M5
Hampton Cres., D.L.	58	P14
Hampton Est. 3	38	Q5
Hampton Grn. 7	34	G6
Hampton Pk., D.L.	58	P15
Hanbury La. 8	43	J9
Hannaville Pk. 6	48	H13
Hanover La. 8	43	J9
Hanover Quay 2	44	M9
Hanover Sq. W. 8	43	J9
Hanover La.		
Hanover St. E. 2	44	L9
Hanover St. W. 8	43	J9
Ash St.		
Harbour Ct. 1	43	K8
Marlborough St.		
Harbour Rd., Howth	31	AA2
Harbour Ter., D.L.	60	U15
Harbour Vw., Howth	31	BB3
St. Lawrence Rd.		
Harbourmaster Pl. 1	44	L8
Harcourt Grn. 2	49	K11
Harcourt La. 2	43	K10
Harcourt Rd.		
Harcourt Rd. 2	43	K10
Harcourt St. 2	43	K10
Harcourt Ter. 2	43	K10
Harcourt Ter. La. 2	50	L11
Hardbeck Av. 12	46	D12
Hardiman Rd. 9	35	K5
Hardwicke Pl. 1	35	K7
Hardwicke St. 1	35	K7
Harlech Cres. 14	57	N15
Harlech Downs 14	57	N15
Harlech Gro. 14	57	N15
Harlech Vills. 14	57	N15
Harman St. 8	42	H10
Harmonstown Rd. 5	26	Q4
Harmonstown Sta. 5	26	Q4
Harmony Av. 4	50	M12
Harmony Row 2	44	M9
Harold Rd. 7	42	H8
Harolds Cross Rd. 6	48	H13
Haroldville Av. 8	42	H10
Harrington St. 8	43	K10
Harrison Row 6	49	J13
Harry St. 2	43	K9
Harty Av. 12	47	E12
Harty Ct. 12	47	E12
Harty Pl. 8	43	J10
Harvard 14	57	N15
Hastings St. 4	45	N9
Hatch La. 2	44	L10
Hatch Pl. 2	44	L10
Hatch St. Lwr.		
Hatch St. Lwr. 2	44	L10
Hatch St. Upper 2	43	K10
Havelock Pl. 4	45	N10
Bath Av.		
Havelock Sq. E. 4	45	N10
Havelock Sq. N. 4	45	N10
Havelock Sq. S. 4	45	N10
Havelock Sq. W. 4	45	N10
Havelock Ter. 4	45	N10
Bath Av.		
Haven, The 9	23	K4
Haverty Rd. 3	37	N6
Hawkins St. 2	44	L8
Hawthorn Av. 3	44	M8
Hawthorn Manor, D.L.	59	R16
Hawthorn Ter. 3	36	M7
Hayden Sq., Stillorgan	57	O15
Haymarket 7	43	J8
Hazel Pk. 12	48	G13
Hazel Rd. 9	37	N5
Hazelbrook Ct. 6	48	H13
Hazelbrook Dr. 6	48	G13
Hazelbrook Pk., Tallaght	52	C15
Hazelbrook Rd. 6	48	G13
Hazelcroft Gdns. 11	22	G4
Hazelcroft Rd.		
Hazelcroft Pk. 11	22	G4
Hazelcroft Rd.		
Hazelcroft Rd. 11	22	G4
Hazeldean 4	51	N12
Hazelwood Ct. 5	25	O3
Hazelwood Dr. 5	25	O3
Hazelwood Gro. 5	25	O3
Hazelwood Pk. 5	25	O3
Headford Gro. 14	55	K16
Healthfield Rd. 6	49	J13
Healy St. 1	36	L7
Rutland Pl. N.		
Heath, The 6	53	F15
Heath Cres. 7	33	E5
Heath Gro. 7	33	F5
Heathfield, D.L.	60	T16
Heidelberg 14	57	N15
Hellers Copse, Stillorgan	58	Q16
Hendrick La. 7	42	H8
Benburb St.		
Hendrick Pl. 7	42	H8
Hendrick St. 7	43	J8
Henley Ct. 14	56	L15
Henley Pk. 14	56	L15
Henley Vills. 14	56	L15
Henrietta La. 1	43	K8
Henrietta Pl. 1	43	J8
Henrietta St. 1	43	J8
Henry Pl. 1	43	K8
Henry St. 1	43	K8
Herbert Av. 4	63	P13
Herbert Cotts. 4	51	N11
Herbert La. 2	44	M10
Herbert Pk. 4	50	M11
Herbert Pl. 2	44	M10
Herbert Rd. 4	45	N10
Herbert St. 2	44	L10
Herberton Dr. 12	42	G10
Herberton Pk. 8	42	G10
Herberton Rd. 8	42	G10
Herberton Rd. 12	42	G10
Heuston Sta. 8	42	G8
Hewardine Ter. 1	36	L7
Killarney St.		
Heytesbury La. 4	50	M11
Heytesbury Pl. 8	43	J10
Long La.		
Heytesbury St. 8	43	K10
Hibernian Av. 3	36	M7
High Pk. 9	24	M4
High Sch. of Domestic Economy, D.L.	58	Q14
High St. 8	43	J9
Highfield Ct. 6	49	J13
Highfield Gro. 6	49	K13
Highfield Pk. 14	56	L15
Highfield Rd. 6	49	J13
Highthorn Pk., D.L.	60	U17
Hill, The, D.L.	60	U16
Hill, The, Stillorgan	58	Q16
Hill St. 1	35	K7
Hillcrest 12	53	F16
Hillcrest Pk. 11	23	J3
Hillsbrook Av. 12	47	E13
Hillsbrook Cres. 12	47	E13
Hillsbrook Dr. 12	47	F13
Hillsbrook Gro. 12	47	E13
Hillside Dr. 14	55	J15
Hillside Vw., Howth	28	U3
Hoeys Ct. 2	43	K9
Castle St.		
Hogan Av. 2	44	M9
Hogan Pl. 2	44	M9
Holles Row 2	44	M9
Holles St. 2	44	L9
Holly Rd. 9	37	N5
Hollybank Av. 6	50	L12
Hollybank Rd. 9	35	K6
Hollybrook Ct. 3	37	O6
Hollybrook Rd.		
Hollybrook Ct. Dr. 3	37	O6
Hollybrook Gro. 3	37	N6
Hollybrook Pk. 3	37	O6
Hollybrook Rd. 3	37	O6
Hollywood Dr. 14	57	N16
Hollywood Pk. 14	57	N16
Holmston Av., D.L.	61	V17
Holy Cross Coll. 3	36	L6
Holycross Av. 3	36	L6
Holyrood Pk. 4	51	O11
Holywell Cres. 5	27	S2
Holywell Rd. 5	27	S2
Home Fm. Pk. 9	36	L5
Home Fm. Rd. 9	23	K4
Home Vills. 4	50	M11
Homeville 6	49	K12
Hope Av. 3	36	M7
Hope St. 4	44	M9
Hopkins Sq., Stillorgan	57	O15
Horseman's Row 1	43	K8
Parnell St.		
Horton Ct. 6	54	H14
Hotel Yd. 1	43	K8
House of Retreat 8	41	E10
Howard St. 4	44	M9
Howth Castle, Howth	31	AA3
Howth Golf Course, Howth	30	Z4
Howth Junct. 5	28	T2

Howth Rd. 3	37	N6	
Howth Rd., Howth	30	Z2	
Howth Sta., Howth	31	AA2	
Howth Vw. Pk. 5	27	S2	
Huband Bri. 4	44	M10	
Huband Rd. 12	46	D11	
Hudson Rd., D.L.	61	W17	
Hughes Rd. E. 12	47	E12	
Hughes Rd. N. 12	47	E12	
Hughes Rd. S. 12	47	E12	
Hume St. 2	44	L10	
Huttons Pl. 1	36	L7	
Huxley Cres. 8	42	H10	
Hyacinth St. 3	36	M7	
Hyde Pk. 6	54	G15	
Hyde Pk. Av., D.L.	58	Q15	
Hyde Pk. Gdns., Blackrock	58	Q15	
Hyde Sq., Stillorgan	57	O15	

I

Idrone Ter., D.L.	59	R15	
Imaal Rd. 7	34	H6	
Inchicore Rd. 8	41	F9	
Inchicore Sq. 8	41	E9	
Inchicore Ter. N. 8	41	E9	
Inchicore Ter. S. 8	41	E9	
Incorporated Dental Hosp. of Ireland 2	44	L9	
Incorporated Orthopaedic Hosp. 3	38	P6	
Infirmary Rd. 7	42	G8	
Ingram Rd. 8	43	J10	
Innisfallen Par. 7	35	K6	
Innishmaan Rd. 9	24	L4	
Innismore 12	47	F12	
Inns Quay 7	43	J9	
Inver Rd. 7	34	G6	
Invermore Gro. 5	27	S2	
Carraroe Av.			
Inverness Rd. 3	36	M6	
Iona Cres. 9	35	K6	
Iona Dr. 9	35	K6	
Iona Pk. 9	35	K6	
Iona Rd. 9	35	J6	
Iona Vills. 9	35	K6	
Iris Gro., Stillorgan	57	O15	
Irishtown Rd. 4	45	N9	
Irvine Cres. 3	44	M8	
Church Rd.			
Irvine Ter. 3	44	M8	
Irwin Ct. 8	42	G9	
Irwin St. 8	42	G9	
Island St. 8	42	H9	
Island Vill. 2	44	M9	
Hogan Av.			
Islington Av., D.L.	61	V16	
Isolda Rd. 4	45	O9	
Ivar St. 7	42	H8	
Iveagh Bldgs. 8	43	J10	
Kevin St. Upper			
Iveagh Gdns. 12	47	F11	
Iveleary Rd. 9	24	L4	
Iveragh Ct. 4	45	N10	
Iveragh Rd. 9	24	L3	
Ivy Ter. 8	42	H10	

J

James Joyce Ct., Kilbarrack	29	U3	
James Larkin Rd. 3	39	S5	
James Larkin Rd. 5	39	S5	
James McCormack Gdns., Sutton	29	W2	
James Pl. 8	41	E9	
James Pl. E. 2	44	L10	
James St. N. 3	36	M7	
James's Gate 8	42	H9	
James's St.			
James's St. 8	42	H9	
James's St. E. 2	44	L10	
Jamestown Av. 8	40	D10	
Jamestown Rd. (Inchicore) 8	40	D10	
Jamestown Rd. (Finglas) 11	22	G2	
Jane Ville, D.L.	60	U16	
Tivoli Rd.			

Jerome Connor Pl. 7	42	G8	
Sullivan St.			
Jervis La. Lwr. 1	43	K8	
Jervis La. Upper 1	43	K8	
Jervis St. 1	43	K8	
Jetty Rd. 1	62	P8	
John Dillon St. 8	43	J9	
John F. Kennedy Dr. 12	46	C11	
John McCormack Av. 12	47	E12	
John St. S. 8	43	J9	
John St. W. 8	43	J9	
Johns La. W. 8	43	J9	
Johnsons Ct. 2	43	K9	
Grafton St.			
Johnsons Pl. 2	43	K9	
King St. S.			
Johnstown Pk. 11	23	J3	
Jones's Rd. 3	36	L7	
Josephine Av. 7	35	K7	
Leo St.			
Joshua La. 2	43	K9	
Dawson St.			
Joy St. 4	44	M9	
Barrow St.			
Joyce Rd. 9	35	K5	
Jumping Grd. 4	51	N11	

K

Keadeen Av., Tallaght	52	C14	
Kearns Pl. 8	42	G9	
Keeper Rd. 12	42	G10	
Kells Rd. 12	48	G12	
Kelly's Av., D.L.	61	U15	
Kelly's Row 1	35	K7	
Dorset St. Lwr.			
Kellys Row 1	35	K7	
Kempton Av. 7	33	E5	
Kempton Ct. 7	33	E5	
Kempton Grn. 7	33	E5	
Kempton Gro. 7	33	E5	
Kempton Heath 7	33	E5	
Kempton Lawn 7	33	E5	
Kempton Pk. 7	33	E5	
Kempton Ri. 7	33	E5	
Kempton Vw. 7	33	E5	
Kempton Way 7	33	E5	
Kenilworth La. 6	49	J12	
Kenilworth Pk. 6	48	H12	
Kenilworth Rd. 6	49	J12	
Kenilworth Sq. E. 6	49	J12	
Kenilworth Sq. N. 6	49	J12	
Kenilworth Sq. S. 6	49	J12	
Kenilworth Sq. W. 6	49	J12	
Kenkworth La. 6	49	J12	
Kenmare Par. 1	35	K7	
Dorset St. Lwr.			
Kennedy Village 8	42	G9	
Kennington Clo., Tallaght	52	D15	
Kennington Cres., Tallaght	52	D15	
Kennington Lawn, Tallaght	53	E15	
Kennington Rd., Tallaght	52	D15	
Keogh Sq. 8	41	F9	
Kerlogue Rd. 4	45	O10	
Kevin St. Lwr. 8	43	K10	
Kevin St. Upper 8	43	J10	
Kickam Rd. 8	41	F9	
Kilakea Clo. 12	52	C14	
Tibradden Dr.			
Kilakea Dr. 12	52	C14	
Tibradden Dr.			
Kilbarrack Av. 5	28	U3	
Kilbarrack Gdns. 5	28	U3	
Kilbarrack Gro. 5	28	T3	
Kilbarrack Par., Kilbarrack	28	T2	
Kilbarrack Rd. 5	27	S2	
Kilbarrack Sta. 5	28	T3	
Kilbarrack Way, Kilbarrack	28	T2	
Kilbarron Av. 5	25	N2	
Kilbarron Dr. 5	25	N2	
Kilbarron Pk. 5	25	N2	
Kilbarron Rd. 5	25	N2	

Kilbride Rd. 5	38	P5	
Kildare Pk. 12	47	F11	
Kildare Rd. 12	47	F11	
Kildare St. 2	44	L9	
Kildonan Av. 11	21	F2	
Kildonan Dr. 11	21	F2	
Kildonan Rd. 11	21	F2	
Kilfenora Dr. 5	27	S2	
Kilfenora Rd. 12	48	G12	
Kilkieran Ct. 7	34	G5	
Kilkieran Rd. 7	34	G5	
Kill Abbey, D.L.	60	S17	
Killala Rd. 7	34	G5	
Killan Rd. 3	44	M8	
Killarney Av. 1	36	L7	
Killarney Par. 7	35	K6	
Killarney St. 1	36	L7	
Killary Gro. 5	27	S2	
Ardara Av.			
Killeen Rd. 6	49	K12	
Killester Abbey 5	26	P4	
Killester Av. 5	26	O4	
Killester Ct. 5	26	P4	
Killester Pk. 5	26	P4	
Killester Sta. 5	38	P5	
Kilmacud Pk., Stillorgan	57	O16	
Kilmacud Rd. Lwr. 14	57	N16	
Kilmacud Rd. Upper 14	56	M16	
Kilmainham Bri. 8	41	F9	
Kilmainham La. 8	41	F9	
Kilmashogue Clo. 12	52	D14	
Kilmashogue Dr.			
Kilmashogue Dr. 12	52	D14	
Kilmashogue Gro. 12	52	C14	
Kilmore Av. 5	25	O2	
Kilmore Clo. 5	25	O2	
Kilmore Cres. 5	26	P2	
Kilmore Dr. 5	25	O2	
Kilmore Rd. 5	25	O3	
Kilmorony Clo. 5	27	S2	
Kilnamanagh Rd. 12	46	D12	
Kilohan Gro. 12	52	D14	
Kilrock La., Howth	31	BB3	
Kilshane Rd. 11	21	E3	
Kilvere 14	54	G15	
Kilworth Rd. 12	47	E11	
Kimmage Ct. 6	48	G13	
Kimmage Gro. 6	48	H13	
Kimmage Rd. Lwr. 6	48	G13	
Kimmage Rd. W. 12	47	F13	
Kinahan St. 7	42	G8	
Kincora Av. 3	37	O6	
Kincora Ct. 3	38	Q7	
Kincora Dr. 3	38	P6	
Kincora Gro. 3	38	P6	
Kincora Pk. 3	38	P6	
Kincora Rd. 3	38	P6	
King St. N. 7	43	J8	
King St. S. 2	43	K9	
Kingram La. 2	44	L10	
Kings Av. 1	36	M7	
Kings Hall 8	40	D8	
Kings Inns St. 1	43	K8	
Kingsland Par. 8	49	K11	
Kingsland Pk. Av. 8	43	K10	
Kinvara Av. 7	33	F5	
Kinvara Dr. 7	33	E5	
Kinvara Gro. 7	33	E5	
Kinvara Pk. 7	33	E5	
Kinvara Rd. 7	33	E5	
Kippure Av. 12	52	C14	
Kippure Pk. 11	21	F4	
Kirkwood 4	51	O11	
Kirwan St. 7	42	H8	
Kirwan St. Cotts. 7	42	H8	
Kirwan St.			
Kitestown Rd., Howth	31	BB4	
Knapton Ct., D.L.	60	U16	
Vesey Pl.			
Knapton Lawn, D.L.	60	U16	
Knapton Rd.			
Knapton Rd., D.L.	60	U16	
Knights Bri. 3	38	P6	
Knockcullen Pk. 14	53	F16	
Knocklyon Av. 14	53	E16	
Knocklyon Dr. 14	53	F16	
Knocklyon Pk. 14	53	E16	
Knocknarea Av. 12	47	F11	
Knocknarea Rd. 12	47	E11	

Knocknashee 14	57	N1	
Kyber Rd. 8	33	E	
Kyle-Clare Rd. 4	45	O	
Kylemore Av. 10	40	C1	
Kylemore Dr. 10	40	C1	
Kylemore Pk. N. 10	40	C1	
Kylemore Pk. S. 10	40	C1	
Kylemore Pk. W. 10	40	C1	
Kylemore Rd. 10	40	C	

L

La Touche Dr. 12	40	D1	
La Touche Rd. 12	46	D1	
La Vista Av., Howth	30	Y	
Laburnum Rd. 14	50	M1	
Lad La. 2	44	L1	
Lagan Rd. 11	22	G	
Lakelands, The 14	55	J1	
Lakelands Pk. 6	54	H1	
Lally Rd. 10	40	D	
Lambay Rd. 9	23	K	
Lambourne Village 3	38	P	
Lambs Ct. 8	42	H	
James's St.			
Landen Rd. 10	40	C1	
Landscape Av. 14	55	K1	
Landscape Cres. 14	55	K1	
Landscape Gdns. 14	55	K1	
Landscape Pk. 14	55	K1	
Landscape Rd. 14	55	K1	
Lanesville, D.L.	60	T1	
Langrishe Pl. 1	36	L	
Summerhill			
Lansdown Valley Pk. 12	41	E1	
Lansdowne Gdns. 4	45	N1	
Shelbourne Rd.			
Lansdowne Hall 4	45	N1	
Tritonville Rd.			
Lansdowne La. 4	45	N1	
Lansdowne Pk. 4	44	M1	
Lansdowne Pk. 14	53	F1	
Lansdowne Rd. 4	45	N1	
Lansdowne Rd. Sta. 4	45	N1	
Lansdowne Ter. 4	51	N1	
Serpentine Av.			
Lansdowne Valley Cres. 12	41	E1	
Kilworth Rd.			
Lansdowne Valley Rd. 12	46	D1	
Lansdowne Village 4	45	N1	
Laracor Gdns. 5	27	S	
Laragh Clo. 5	27	S	
Laragh Gro. 5	27	S	
Laragh Clo.			
Larch Gro. 6	50	L1	
Larchfield 14	56	M1	
Larchfield Pk. 14	56	M1	
Larchfield Rd. 14	56	M1	
Larkfield Av. 6	48	H1	
Larkfield Gdns. 6	48	H1	
Larkfield Gro. 6	48	H1	
Larkfield Rd. 6	48	H1	
Larkhill Rd. 9	24	L	
Lauders La., Baldoyle	29	X	
Laundry La. 6	49	J1	
Laurel Av. 14	56	L1	
Laurel Dr. 14	56	L1	
Laurel Hill, D.L.	61	U1	
Laurel Rd. 14	56	L1	
Laurels, The 6	48	H1	
Laurels, The 14	56	L1	
Laurelton 6	55	J1	
Lavarna Gro. 6	54	G1	
Lavarna Rd. 6	48	G1	
Lavista Av. (Killester) 5	38	P	
Lawn, The 11	22	G	
Lawrence Gro. 3	37	O	
Le Bas Ter. 6	49	J1	
Leinster Rd. W.			
Le Vere Ter. 6	49	J1	
Lea Cres. 4	51	O1	
Lea Rd. 4	51	O1	
Leahys Ter. 4	45	O1	
Lee Rd. 11	34	H	
Leeson Clo. 2	44	L1	
Leeson La. 2	44	L1	

72

Name		
eeson Pk. 6	50	L11
eeson Pk. Av. 6	50	L11
eeson Pl. 2	44	L10
eeson St. Bri. 2	50	L11
eeson St. Lwr. 2	44	L10
eeson St. Upper 4	50	L11
eeson Village 6	50	L11
eighlin Rd. 12	48	G12
ein Gdns.	26	Q4
(Gairdin Lein) 5		
in Pk. 15	26	Q3
in Rd. 5	26	Q3
einster Av. 3	36	M7
einster La. 2	44	L9
Leinster St. S.		
einster Lawn 14	56	M14
einster Mkt. 2	43	K8
D'Olier St.		
inster Pl. 6	49	J12
inster Rd. 6	49	J12
inster Rd. W. 6	49	J12
inster Sq. 6	49	K12
inster St. 2	44	L9
inster St. E. 3	36	M7
inster St. N. 7	35	J6
inster St. S. 2	44	M10
itrim Pl. 4	44	M10
Grand Canal St. Upper		
ix Rd. 7	34	H6
land Pl. 1	44	M8
mon St. 2	43	K9
nnox Pl. 8	49	K11
nnox St. 8	49	K11
ntisk Lawn 5	27	S2
o Av. 7	35	K7
Leo St.		
o St. 7	35	K7
slies Bldgs. 7	35	J7
ukos Rd. 4	45	O9
perty La. 8	43	K10
orary Rd., D.L.	61	U16
fey St. 10	41	E9
fey St. Lwr. 1	43	K8
fey St. Upper 1	43	K8
fey St. W. 7	43	J9
Benburb St.		
ne St. 2	44	M9
nekiln Clo. 12	53	E14
nekiln Dr. 12	53	E14
nekiln Gro. 12	47	E13
nekiln La. 12	53	E14
nekiln Pk. 12	53	E14
nekiln Rd. 12	52	D14
newood Av. 5	27	R2
newood Pk. 5	27	R2
newood Rd. 5	27	R2
coln La. 12	43	J8
coln Pl. 2	44	L9
den Gro.,	58	Q16
tillorgan		
den Vale,	59	R16
tillorgan		
dsay Rd. 9	35	J6
enhall Par. 7	43	J8
enhall Ter. 7	43	J8
enhall St. 1	61	W17
k Rd., D.L.	61	W17
ourn St. 7	43	J8
cannor Rd. 7	34	G5
e Rd. 12	47	E12
more Rd. 12	48	G12
sadel Av. 12	47	F11
sadel Ct. 12	47	F11
sadel Dr. 12	47	F11
sadel Rd. 12	47	F11
senfield 6	49	K11
en La. 1	43	K8
le Britain St. 1	43	J8
le Longford St. 2	43	K9
tus La. 1	43	K8
nbard Ct. 2	44	L9
nbard St. E. 2	44	L9
nbard St. W. 8	43	J10
nond Av. 3	36	M6
donbridge Dr. 4	45	N10
ondonbridge Rd.		
donbridge Rd. 4	45	N10
g La. 7	35	K7
g La.	43	J10
enter Flds.) 8		
Long La. Gro. 8	43	J10
Long Mile Rd. 12	46	C12
Longford La. 8	43	K9
Longford St. Great		
Longford Pl., D.L.	60	U16
Longford St. Great 8	43	K9
Longford St. Little 2	43	K10
Digges St.		
Longford Ter., D.L.	60	T16
Longs Pl. 8	42	H9
Longwood Av. 8	49	J11
Longwood Pk. 14	55	J16
Lorcan Av. 9	24	M2
Lorcan Cres. 9	24	M2
Lorcan Dr. 9	24	M2
Lorcan Grn. 9	25	N2
Lorcan Grn. 9	24	M2
Lorcan O'Toole Pk. 12	47	F13
Lorcan Pk. 9	24	M2
Lorcan Rd. 9	24	M2
Lorcan Vills. 9	25	N2
Lord Edward St. 2	43	K9
Lord's Wk. 8	33	F7
Loreto Av. 14	55	J16
Loreto Ct. 14	55	J16
Loreto Cres. 14	55	J16
Loreto Pk. 14	55	J16
Loreto Rd. 8	42	H10
Loreto Row 14	55	J16
Loreto Ter. 14	55	J16
Lorne Ter. 8	42	G9
Brookfield Rd.		
Lotts 1	43	K8
Lough Derg Rd. 5	27	R4
Lourdes Rd. 8	42	H10
Louvain 14	57	N15
Louvain Glade 14	57	N15
Love La. E. 2	44	M10
Lower Churchtown	56	L14
Rd. 14		
Lower Dodder Rd. 14	54	H14
Lower Glen Rd.,	32	C7
Castleknock		
Luby Rd. 8	41	F9
Lugnaquilla Av. 12	52	C14
Luke St. 2	44	L8
Lullymore Ter. 8	48	H11
Lurgan St. 7	43	J8
Lynchs La. 10	40	C9
Lynchs Pl. 7	35	J7
Lyndon Gate 7	33	F6

M

Name		
Mabbot La. 1	44	L8
Mabel St. 3	36	L6
Macken St. 2	44	M9
Macken Vills. 2	44	M9
Mackies Pl. 2	44	L10
Madeleine Ter. 8	41	E9
Madison Rd. 8	42	G10
Magennis Pl. 2	44	L9
Magenta Cres. 9	24	M2
Magenta Hall 9	24	M2
Magenta Pl., D.L.	61	V17
Mageough Home 6	50	L13
Maginnis Sq. 2	44	L9
Pearse St.		
Mahers Pl. 2	44	M9
Macken St.		
Maiden Row,	40	C8
Chapelizod		
Main St. 5	27	R4
Main St. (Finglas) 11	22	G3
Main St.	56	L16
(Dundrum) 14		
Main St.	54	H15
(Rathfarnham) 14		
Main St., Blackrock	59	R15
Main St., Howth	31	BB3
Malachi Rd. 7	42	H8
Malahide Rd. 3	37	N6
Malahide Rd. 5	26	O4
Mallin Av. 8	42	H10
Malone Gdns. 4	45	N10
Malpas Pl. 8	43	J10
Malpas St.		
Malpas St. 8	43	J10
Malpas Ter. 8	43	J10
Malpas St.		
Mander's Ter. 6	50	L11
Ranelagh Rd.		
Mangerton Rd. 12	47	E11
Mannix Rd. 9	35	K5
Manor Av. 6	54	G14
Manor Pl. 7	42	H8
Manor St. 7	42	H8
Mansion Ho. 2	44	L9
Maolbuille Rd. 11	23	K3
Maple Dr. 6	48	H13
Maple Rd. 14	50	M13
Maples, The 14	56	M14
Maples, The, D.L.	60	T16
Maquay Bri. 2	44	M10
Maretimo Gdns. E.,	59	S15
D.L.		
Maretimo Gdns. W.,	59	S15
D.L.		
Newtown Av.		
Maretimo Pl., D.L.	59	S15
Newtown Av.		
Maretimo Rd., D.L.	59	S15
Newtown Av.		
Maretimo Vills., D.L.	59	S15
Margaret Pl. 4	45	N10
Marguerite Rd. 9	35	K5
Marian Cres. 14	54	G16
Marian Dr. 14	54	G15
Marian Gro. 14	54	H16
Marian Pk.	54	G16
(Rathfarnham) 14		
Marian Pk., Baldoyle	29	U2
Marian Rd. 14	54	G16
Marine Av., D.L.	61	W17
Marine Ct., D.L.	61	W17
Marine Dr. 4	45	O10
Marine Par., D.L.	61	W17
Marine Rd., D.L.	61	V16
Mariners Cove, Howth	31	BB3
Marino Av. 3	37	N6
Marino Cres. 3	37	N6
Marino Grn. 3	37	N6
Marino Mart 3	37	N6
Marino Pk. 3	36	M6
Marino Pk. Av. 3	37	N6
Marion Vills. 8	42	H10
Mark St. 2	44	L9
Market St. S. 8	42	H9
Marks All. W. 8	43	J9
Marks La. 2	44	L9
Marlborough Ms. 7	34	G7
Marlborough Pl. 1	44	L8
Marlborough Rd.	50	L12
(Donnybrook) 4		
Marlborough Rd. 6	50	L12
Marlborough Rd. 7	34	G7
Marlborough St. 1	43	K8
Marlborough Vw. 7	35	J7
Marrowbone La. 8	42	H10
Marrowbone La. Ct. 8	42	H9
Marshalsea La. 8	42	H9
Martello Av., D.L.	61	V16
Martello Ms. 4	63	P12
Martello Ter., D.L.	58	Q14
Martello Vw. 4	45	O10
Martello Wd. 4	63	P11
Martin Savage Pk.,	32	D5
Ashtown		
Martin Savage Rd. 7	33	E6
Martin St. 8	49	K11
Martins Row,	40	C8
Chapelizod		
Mary St. 1	43	K8
Mary St. Little 7	43	K8
Maryfield Av. 5	25	O3
Maryfield Cres. 5	25	O3
Maryfield Dr. 5	25	O3
Mary's Abbey 7	43	K8
Mary's La. 7	43	J8
Maryville Rd. 5	26	Q4
Mask Av. 5	26	P3
(Ascal Measc) 5		
Mask Cres. 5	26	P3
Mask Dr. 5	26	P3
Mask Grn. 5	26	P3
Mask Rd. 5	26	P3
Masonic Sch. 4	51	N11
Mastersons La. 2	43	K10
Charlemont St.		
Mater Misericordiae	35	K7
Hosp. 7		
Mather Rd. N.,	57	O15
Stillorgan		
Mather Rd. S.,	57	O15
Stillorgan		
Maunsell Pl. 7	35	K7
Mountjoy St.		
Maxwell Rd. 6	49	K12
Maxwell St. 8	42	H10
May La. 7	43	J8
May St. 3	36	L6
Mayfield 6	55	J14
Mayfield Rd.	48	H13
(Terenure) 6		
Mayfield Rd.	42	G10
(Kilmainham) 8		
Mayola Ct. 14	56	L15
Mayor St. Lwr. 1	44	M8
Mayor St. Upper 1	44	M8
Maywood Av. 5	27	S4
Maywood Clo. 5	27	S4
Maywood Cres. 5	27	S4
Maywood Dr. 5	27	S4
Maywood Gro. 5	27	S4
Maywood La. 5	27	S4
Maywood Pk. 5	27	S4
Maywood Rd. 5	27	S4
McAuley Av.	26	Q3
(Ascal Mac Amhlaoi) 5		
McAuley Dr. 5	26	Q3
McAuley Pk. 5	26	Q4
McAuley Rd. 5	26	Q3
McCabe Vills.,	58	P14
Booterstown		
McCarthy's Bldgs. 7	35	J6
Cabra Rd.		
McDonald Av. 8	42	G9
McKee Av. 11	22	G2
McKee Barracks 7	34	G7
McKee Dr. 7	34	G7
McKee Pk. 7	34	G7
McKee Rd. 11	22	H2
McMahon St. 8	43	J10
McMorrough Rd. 6	49	J13
Meades Ter. 2	44	M9
Meadow Pk. 14	55	K16
Meadow Pk. Av. 14	55	K16
Meadowbank 6	55	J14
Meadowbrook Av.,	29	V2
Howth		
Meadowbrook	29	V2
Lawn, Howth		
Meadowbrook Pk.,	29	V2
Howth		
Meadows, The 5	26	Q4
Meath Hosp. 8	43	J10
Meath Pl. 8	43	J9
Meath Sq. 8	43	J9
Meath St.		
Meath St. 8	43	J9
Meehan Sq.,	57	O14
Stillorgan		
Meetinghouse La. 7	43	K8
Mary's Abbey		
Mellifont Av., D.L.	61	V16
Mellowes Av. 11	21	F2
Mellowes Ct. 11	22	G3
Mellowes Cres. 11	22	G3
Mellowes Pk. 11	21	F2
Mellowes Rd. 11	21	F2
Melrose Av. 3	36	M6
Melvin Rd. 6	48	H13
Memorial Rd. 1	44	L8
Mercer St. Lwr. 2	43	K9
Mercer St. Upper 2	43	K10
Merchamp 3	38	Q6
Merchants Quay 8	43	J9
Merchants Rd. 3	45	N8
Merlyn Dr. 4	51	O12
Merlyn Pk. 4	51	O12
Merlyn Rd. 4	51	O12
Merrion Cres.,	63	P13
Booterstown		
Merrion Gro., D.L.	58	P14
Merrion Pk., D.L.	58	P15
Merrion Pl. 2	44	L9
Merrion Rd. 4	51	N11
Merrion Row 2	44	L10
Merrion Sq. E. 2	44	L9

Name	Pg	Grid
Merrion Sq. N. 2	44	L9
Merrion Sq. S. 2	44	L9
Merrion Sq. W. 2	44	L9
Merrion Strand 4	63	P12
Merrion Sq. Lwr. 2	44	L9
Clare St.		
Merrion Sq. Upper 2	44	L10
Merrion Vw. Av. 4	51	O12
Merrion Village 4	63	P12
Merton Av. 8	42	H10
Merton Dr. 6	50	L12
Merton Rd. 6	50	L13
Merville Av.	36	M6
(Fairview) 3		
Mespil Rd. 4	44	L10
Mews, The 3	38	P6
Mews, The	39	R6
(Dollymount) 3		
Middle Third 5	38	P5
Military Cem. 7	34	G6
Military Rd.	49	K11
(Rathmines) 6		
Military Rd.	42	G9
(Kilmainham) 8		
Military Rd.	40	D8
(Phoenix Pk.) 8		
Mill La. 8	43	J10
Newmarket		
Mill La., Ashtown	32	D5
Mill St. 8	43	J10
Millbourne Av. 9	35	K5
Millbrook Av. 5	27	R2
Millbrook Ct. 8	42	G9
Millbrook Dr. 5	27	S2
Millbrook Gro. 5	27	R2
Millbrook Pk. 5	27	R3
Millbrook Rd. 5	27	R2
Millbrook Village 6	50	M13
Prospect La.		
Millbrook Vills. 5	27	R2
Millgate Dr. 12	53	E14
Millmount Av. 9	35	K5
Millmount Gro. 14	56	L14
Millmount Pl. 9	36	L5
Millmount Ter.	36	L5
(Drumcondra) 9		
Millmount Av.		
Millmount Ter.	56	L14
(Dundrum) 14		
Millmount Gro.		
Millmount Vills. 9	35	K5
Milltown Bri. Rd. 14	50	L13
Milltown Dr. 14	55	K15
Milltown Gro. 14	55	K15
Milltown Hill 6	50	L13
Milltown Rd.		
Milltown Path 6	50	L13
Milltown Rd. 6	50	L13
Misery Hill 2	44	M9
Moatfield Av. 5	26	Q3
Moatfield Pk. 5	26	Q2
Moatfield Rd. 5	26	Q2
Moeran Rd. 12	47	E12
Moira Rd. 7	42	H8
Moland Pl. 1	44	L8
Talbot St.		
Molesworth Pl. 2	44	L9
Molesworth St.		
Molesworth St. 2	44	L9
Molyneux Rd. 8	43	J9
Monasterboice Rd. 12	48	G11
Monck Pl. 7	35	J7
Monkstown Av., D.L.	60	T17
Monkstown Cres.,	60	T16
D.L.		
Monkstown Fm., D.L.	60	T17
Monkstown Gate,	60	U16
D.L.		
Monkstown Gro.,	60	T17
D.L.		
Monkstown Rd., D.L.	59	S15
Monkstown Valley,	60	T16
D.L.		
Montague Ct. 2	43	K10
Protestant Row		
Montague La. 2	43	K10
Montague Pl. 2	43	K10
Montague La.		
Montague St. 2	43	K10
Montpelier Dr. 7	42	H8
Montpelier Gdns. 7	42	G8
Montpelier Hill 7	42	G8
Montpelier Par., D.L.	59	S16
Montpelier Pk. 7	42	G8
Montpelier Pl., D.L.	59	S15
Montrose Av. 5	25	N3
Montrose Clo. 5	25	N3
Montrose Ct. 5	25	O3
Montrose Cres. 5	25	O3
Montrose Dr. 5	25	N3
Montrose Gro. 5	25	N3
Montrose Pk. 5	25	N3
Moore La. 1	43	K8
Moore St. 1	43	K8
Morehampton La. 4	50	M11
Morehampton Rd. 4	50	M11
Morehampton Ter. 4	50	M11
Morgan Pl. 7	43	J9
Inns Quay		
Morning Star Av. 7	43	J8
Morning Star Rd. 8	42	H10
Mornington Gro. 5	26	P3
Mornington Rd. 6	50	L12
Morrogh Ter. 3	36	M5
Moss St. 2	44	L8
Mount Albion Rd. 14	55	K16
Mount Albion Ter. 14	56	L16
Mount Annville, D.L.	57	O16
Mount Annville	57	N16
Convent 14		
Mount Annville	57	N16
Lawn 14		
Mount Annville Pk.,	57	O16
D.L.		
Mount Annville Rd. 14	57	N16
Mount Annville Wd.,	57	O16
D.L.		
Mount Argus Clo. 6	48	H12
Mount Argus Ct. 6	48	H12
Mount Argus Cres. 6	48	H12
Mount Argus Grn. 6	48	H12
Mount Argus Pk. 6	48	H12
Mount Argus Rd. 6	48	H12
Mount Argus Ter. 6	48	H12
Mount Argus Vw. 6	48	H12
Mount Argus Way 6	48	H12
Mount Brown 8	42	G9
Mount Carmel Av. 14	56	M15
Mount Carmel	57	N14
Convent 14		
Mount Carmel Hosp.	55	K14
14		
Mount Carmel Pk.,	52	D16
Tallaght		
Mount Carmel Rd. 14	56	M15
Mount Dillon Ct. 5	26	P3
Mount Drummond	49	J11
Av. 6		
Mount Drummond	49	J11
Sq. 6		
Mount Eden Rd. 4	50	M12
Mount Harold Ter. 6	49	J12
Mount Jerome Cem. 6	48	H11
Mount Merrion Av.,	58	P15
D.L.		
Mount Olive Gro. 5	27	S2
Mount Olive Pk. 5	27	S2
Mount Olive Rd. 5	27	S2
Mount Prospect Av. 3	38	Q5
Mount Prospect Dr. 3	38	Q5
Mount Prospect	39	R6
Gro. 3		
Mount Prospect	38	Q6
Lawns 3		
Mount Prospect Pk. 3	38	Q6
Mount Sandford 6	50	M12
Mount Shannon Rd. 8	42	G10
Mount St. Cres. 2	44	M10
Mount St. Lwr. 2	44	M9
Mount St. Upper 2	44	L10
Mount Tallant Av. 6	48	H13
Mount Tallant Ter. 6	48	H13
Harolds Cross Rd.		
Mount Temple Rd. 7	42	H8
Mount Town Lwr.,	60	U17
D.L.		
Mount Town Pk., D.L.	60	U17
Mount Town Upper,	60	T16
D.L.		
Mount Wd., D.L.	60	U17
Mountain Vw. Av. 6	49	J12
Harolds Cross Rd.		
Mountain Vw. Cotts. 6	50	L12
Mountain Vw. Dr. 14	55	K16
Mountain Vw. Pk. 14	55	K16
Mountain Vw. Rd. 6	50	L12
Mountdown Dr. 12	53	E14
Mountdown Pk. 12	53	E14
Mountdown Rd. 12	53	E14
Mountjoy Cotts. 7	35	K6
North Circular Rd.		
Mountjoy Pl. 1	36	L7
Mountjoy Prison 7	35	K6
Mountjoy Prison	35	K6
Cotts. 7		
Cowley Rd.		
Mountjoy Sq. E. 1	36	L7
Mountjoy Sq. N. 1	35	K7
Mountjoy Sq. S. 1	36	L7
Mountjoy Sq. W. 1	35	K7
Mountjoy St. 7	35	K7
Mountjoy St. Middle 7	35	J7
Mountpleasant Av.	49	K11
Lwr. 6		
Mountpleasant Av.	49	K11
Upper 6		
Mountpleasant	49	K11
Bldgs. 6		
Mountpleasant Par. 6	49	K11
Mountpleasant Pl.		
Mountpleasant Pl. 6	49	K11
Mountpleasant Sq. 6	49	K11
Mourne Rd. 12	47	E13
Moy Elta Rd. 3	36	M7
Moyclare Clo.,	29	V2
Baldoyle		
Moyclare Pk.,	29	V2
Baldoyle		
Moyclare Rd.,	29	V2
Baldoyle		
Moyle Rd. 11	34	G5
Moyne Rd. 6	50	L12
Muckross Av. 12	47	E13
Muckross Cres. 12	47	E13
Muckross Dr. 12	47	F13
Muckross Grn. 12	47	F13
Muckross Gro. 12	47	E13
Muckross Par. 7	35	K6
Killarney Par.		
Muckross Pk. 12	47	E13
Mulgrave St., D.L.	61	V16
Mulgrave Ter., D.L.	61	V16
Mulroy Rd. 7	34	H6
Mulvey Pk. 14	56	M15
Munster St. 7	35	J6
Murrays Cotts. 10	41	E9
Sarsfield Rd.		
Murtagh Rd. 7	42	H8
Muskerry Rd. 10	40	C9
Myra Cotts. 8	41	F9
Myrtle Av., D.L.	61	V17
Myrtle Pk., D.L.	61	V17

N

Nanikin Av. 5	27	R4
Nash St. 8	40	D10
Nashville Pk., Howth	31	BB3
Nashville Rd., Howth	31	BB3
Nassau Pl. 2	44	L9
Nassau St. 2	43	K9
National Maternity	44	M9
Hosp. 2		
National Museum 2	44	L9
Navan Rd.,	20	C4
Castleknock		
Neagh Rd. 6	48	H13
Nelson St. 7	35	K7
Nephin Rd. 7	33	F6
Nerneys Ct. 1	35	K7
New Gra. Rd. 7	34	H6
New Ireland Rd. 8	42	G10
New Lisburn St. 7	43	J8
Coleraine St.		
New Rd. (Inchicore) 8	40	D10
New Rd., Howth	31	BB4
New Rd., The 11	20	C2
New Row S. 8	43	J
New Row Sq. 8	43	J
New St. Gdns. 8	43	J
New St. S. 8	43	J
New Wapping St. 1	44	
Newbridge Av. 4	45	N
Newbridge Dr. 4	45	N
Newbrook Av. 5	28	
Newbrook Rd. 5	28	
Newcomen Av. 3	36	
Newcomen Bri. 3	36	
Newcomen Ct. 3	36	
North Strand Rd.		
Newgrove Av. 4	45	O
Newmarket 8	43	J
Newmarket St. 8	43	J
Newport St. 8	42	
Newtown Av., D.L.	59	R
Newtown Cotts. 5	26	
Newtown Dr. 5	26	
Newtown Pk.,	52	C
Tallaght		
Newtown Vills., D.L.	59	S
Newtownsmith, D.L.	61	W
Niall St. 7	34	
Nicholas Av. 7	43	
Church St.		
Nicholas Pl. 8	43	
Patrick St.		
Nicholas St. 8	43	
Nore Rd. 11	34	
Norfolk Mkt. 1	43	
Parnell St.		
Norfolk Rd. 7	35	
Norseman Pl. 7	42	
North Av., Stillorgan	57	O
North Circular Rd. 1	35	
North Circular Rd. 7	42	
North Great	36	
Clarence St. 1		
North Great Georges	35	
St. 1		
North Rd. 7	33	
North Rd. 8	33	
North Rd. No. 1 1	45	
North Strand Rd. 1	36	
North Strand Rd. 3	36	
North Wall Ext. 1	45	
North Wall Quay 1	44	
Northbrook Av. 5	50	L
Northbrook Av. Lwr. 1	36	L
North Strand Av.		
Northbrook Av.	36	
Upper 3		
Northbrook La. 6	50	L
Northbrook Rd. 6	50	L
Northbrook Ter. 3	36	
Northbrook Vills. 6	50	L
Northbrook Rd.		
Northbrook Wk. 6	50	L
Northcote Av., D.L.	60	L
Northcote Pl., D.L.	60	L
Northland Dr. 11	23	
Northland Gro. 11	22	
Northumberland Av.,	61	V
D.L.		
Northumberland Pk.,	61	V
D.L.		
Northumberland Pl.,	61	V
D.L.		
Northumberland Av.		
Northumberland Rd. 4	44	M
Nortons Av. 7	35	
Norwood Pk. 6	50	M
Nottingham St. 3	36	
Nugent Rd. 14	55	K
Nutgrove Av. 14	55	J
(Ascal An Charrain Chno)		
Nutgrove Pk. 14	56	M
Nutgrove Way 14	55	K
Nutley Av. 4	51	N
Nutley La. 4	51	C
Nutley Pk. 4	51	C
Nutley Rd. 4	51	N
Nutley Sq. 4	51	N

O

Oak Apple Grn. 6	49	
Oak Pk. Av. 9	24	

Name	Page	Grid
Pk. Clo. 9	24	M2
Pk. Dr. 9	24	M2
Pk. Gro. 9	24	M2
Rd. 9	37	N5
lown Rd. 14	55	K16
ield Pl. 8	43	J10
ands Cres. 6	49	K13
ands Dr. 4	51	N11
ands Dr. 6	49	K13
ands Pk. 4	51	N11
ands Ter. 4	51	N11
rpentine Av.		
ands Ter. 6	49	J13
ey Gro., D.L.	59	R16
ey Pk. 3	38	Q6
ey Pk., Stillorgan	59	R16
ey Rd. 6	50	L12
The 3	39	R6
The 14	56	L16
vood Av. 11	22	H2
vood Pk. 11	22	H2
en Rd. 12	47	E12
n's Institute 8	37	N5
en's Pl. N. 9	35	K5
en's Ter. 9	35	J4
spect Av.		
hmines La. 6	49	K11
hmines Rd. Lwr.		
rolan Rd. 8	43	J10
n Pier 1	45	O8
nell Av. 7	35	J7
nell Gdns. 4	45	N10
nell St. Lwr. 1	43	K8
nell St. Upper 1	43	K8
rry Av. 8	43	J10
rry Rd. 8	43	J10
y Rd. 9	35	K5
Lamp Rd. 8	33	E6
vaney Gdns. 7	42	G8
nell Gdns., D.L.	61	V17
noghue St. 8	41	E10
novan Rd. 8	43	J10
novan Rossa 8	43	J9
etavern St.		
y Rd. 7	34	H6
gton Av., Howth	30	Y3
gton Ct., Howth	30	Y3
gton Dr., Howth	30	Y3
gton Lawn, vth	30	Y3
gton Pk., Howth	30	Y2
bag Rd. 10	40	D9
d. 7	42	H8
i. Rd. 14	53	F15
abra Rd. 7	34	G6
amden St. 2	43	K10
court Rd.		
ounty Glen 12	48	G11
ounty Rd. 12	47	F11
unleary, D.L.	60	U16
lmainham 8	42	G9
ill Ct. 8	43	J10
ountpleasant 6	49	K11
entpleasant Pl.		
aas Rd. 12	46	C11
ectory Pk. 14	56	M16
stle Av., Howth	30	Y3
vn Av. 9	23	K2
vn Pk. 9	23	K2
vn Rd. 9	24	L2
ry Rd. 8	41	F10
mount Gro. 14	56	M14
mount Rd. 14	56	M14
Bond St. 8	43	J9
Plunkett Av. (town) 4	45	N9
Plunkett Av.,	60	T17
Plunkett Cres.,	60	T17
er Plunkett Av.		
Plunkett Rd.,	60	T17
Plunkett Sq.,	60	T17
Plunkett Ter.,	60	T17
er Plunkett Rd.		
Oliver Plunkett Vills., D.L.	60	T17
Olney Cres. 6	54	H14
Omni Pk. 9	24	L2
O'Moore Rd. 10	40	D9
O'Neachtain Rd. 9	35	K5
O'Neill's Bldgs. 8	43	K10
Ontario Ter. 6	49	K11
Ophaly Ct. 14	56	M15
O'Quinn Av. 8	42	G9
O'Rahilly Par. 1	43	K8
Moore St.		
Orchard, The 3	36	M6
Orchard, The 5	38	P5
Orchard, The 6	48	G13
Orchard La. 6	50	L11
Orchard Rd. 3	36	M6
Orchard Rd. 5	28	T4
Orchard Rd. S. 6	49	K13
Orchardston 14	54	G16
Orchardstown Av. 14	54	G16
Orchardstown Dr. 14	53	F16
Orchardstown Pk. 14	54	G16
Orchardstown Vills. 14	54	G16
Ordnance Survey Office, Castleknock	32	C6
Ordnance Survey Rd., Castleknock	32	C6
O'Reilly's Av. 8	42	G9
Oriel Pl. 1	36	M7
Oriel St. Lwr. 1	44	M8
Oriel St. Upper 1	44	M8
Ormeau St. 4	45	N9
Ormond Mkt. Sq. 7	43	J9
Ormond Quay Upper		
Ormond Quay Lwr. 1	43	K8
Ormond Quay Upper 7	43	J9
Ormond Sq. 7	43	J8
Ormond St. 8	43	J10
Orpen Clo., Stillorgan	58	Q16
Orpen Dale, Stillorgan	58	Q16
Orpen Grn., Stillorgan	58	Q16
Orwell Gdns. 14	55	K14
Orwell Pk. 6	55	K14
Orwell Pk. Av. 12	53	E15
Orwell Pk. Clo. 12	53	E15
Orwell Pk. Cres. 12	53	F15
Orwell Pk. Dale 12	53	F15
Orwell Pk. Dr. 12	53	F15
Orwell Pk. Glade 12	53	E15
Orwell Pk. Glen 12	53	E15
Orwell Pk. Grn. 12	53	E15
Orwell Pk. Gro. 12	53	E15
Orwell Pk. Hts. 12	53	E15
Orwell Pk. Lawns 12	53	E15
Orwell Pk. Ri. 12	53	E15
Orwell Pk. Vw. 12	53	E15
Orwell Pk. Way 12	53	E15
Orwell Rd. 6	49	J13
Orwell Rd. 14	55	K14
Orwell Wds. 6	55	K14
Oscar Sq. 8	43	J10
Osprey Av., Tallaght	53	E14
Osprey Dr., Tallaght	53	E14
Osprey Lawn, Tallaght	53	E14
Osprey Pk., Tallaght	52	D14
Osprey Rd., Tallaght	53	E15
Ossory Rd. 3	36	M7
Ossory Sq. 8	43	J10
Ostman Pl. 7	42	H8
O'Sullivan Av. 3	36	M7
Oswald Rd. 4	45	O10
Otranto Pl., D.L.	61	W17
Oulton Rd. 3	38	P6
Our Ladys Clo. 8	42	H9
Our Lady's Hospice 6	48	H11
Our Lady's Hosp. 12	47	E11
Our Lady's Rd. 8	42	H10
Ovoca Rd. 8	43	J10
Owendore Av. 14	54	H15
Owendore Cres. 14	54	H15
Owens Av. 8	42	G9
Owenstown Pk., Stillorgan	57	O15
Oxford Rd. 6	49	K11
Oxford Ter. 3	44	M8
Church Rd.		
Oxford Ter. 6	49	K11
Oxford Rd.		
Oxmantown La. 7	42	H8
Blackhall Pl.		
Oxmantown Rd. 7	34	H7
Oxmantown Rd. Lwr. 7	42	H8
Arbour Hill		

P

Name	Page	Grid
Pacelli Av., Baldoyle	28	U3
Packenham, D.L.	60	U16
Paddock, The 7	32	D5
Pairc Baile Munna 11	23	J3
Pairc Clearmont (Claremont Pk.) 4	45	O10
Pakenham Rd., D.L.	60	T16
Pakerton, D.L.	60	U16
Sloperton		
Palace St. 2	43	K9
Dame St.		
Palmerston Gdns. 6	49	K13
Palmerston Gro. 6	50	M13
Palmerston La. 6	50	L13
Palmerston Pk. 6	49	K13
Palmerston Pl. 7	35	J7
Palmerston Rd. 6	49	K13
Palmerston Vills. 6	49	K13
Palms, The 14	57	N15
Paradise Pl. 7	35	K7
Park Av. 4	51	O11
Park Cres. 8	33	F6
Park Cres. 12	47	F13
Park Dr. 6	50	L12
Park La. 4	51	O11
Park La., Chapelizod	40	C8
Park La. E. 2	44	L9
Park Lawn 3	39	R5
Park Pl. 8	41	F9
South Circular Rd.		
Park Rd. 7	33	E5
Park Rd., D.L.	61	V16
Park St. 10	41	E9
Park Ter. 8	43	J9
Park Vw., Castleknock	32	C5
Park Vw. Av. 6	49	K12
Parkgate St. 8	42	H8
Parklands, The 14	55	J15
Parkmore Dr. 6	54	G14
Parkvale, Howth	29	V2
Parkview 7	34	G7
Parkview Av. 6	49	J12
Parliament Row 2	43	K9
Fleet St.		
Parliament St. 2	43	K9
Parnell Av. 12	49	J11
Parnell Rd.		
Parnell Ct. 12	49	J11
Parnell Pl. 1	35	K7
Parnell Rd. 12	42	H10
Parnell Sq. E. 1	35	K7
Parnell Sq. N. 1	35	K7
Parnell Sq. W. 1	43	K8
Parnell St. 1	43	K8
Partridge Ter. 8	40	D10
Patrician Pk., D.L.	60	T17
Patrician Vills., Stillorgan	58	Q16
Patrick Doyle Rd. 14	56	L14
Patrick St. 8	43	J9
Patrick St., D.L.	61	U16
Patricks Clo. S. 8	43	J9
Patricks Row, D.L.	59	R15
Carysfort Av.		
Patrickswell Pl. 11	22	G3
Patriotic Ter. 8	42	G9
Brookfield Rd.		
Pea Fld., D.L.	58	Q15
Pearse Gro. 2	44	M9
Great Clarence Pl.		
Pearse Ho. 2	44	L9
Pearse Sq. E. 2	44	M9
Pearse Sq. N. 2	44	M9
Pearse Sq. W. 2	44	M9
Pearse Sta. 2	44	L9
Pearse St. 2	44	L9
Pembroke Cotts. (Donnybrook) 4	50	M12
Pembroke Cotts. (Ringsend) 4	45	N9
Pembroke Cotts. (Dundrum) 14	56	M16
Pembroke Cotts., D.L.	58	P14
Pembroke Gdns. 4	44	M10
Pembroke La. 2	44	L10
Pembroke La. 4	44	M10
Pembroke Pk. 4	50	M11
Pembroke Pl. 2	44	L10
Pembroke St. Upper		
Pembroke Pl. 4	51	N11
Herbert Pk.		
Pembroke Rd. 4	44	M10
Pembroke Row 2	44	L10
Pembroke St. 4	45	N9
Pembroke St. Lwr. 2	44	L10
Pembroke St. Upper 2	44	L10
Penrose St. 4	45	N9
Percy French Rd. 12	47	E12
Percy La. 4	44	M10
Percy Pl. 4	44	M10
Peter Row 8	43	K9
Peter St. 8	43	K9
Peters Pl. 2	43	K10
Petersons Ct. 2	44	L8
Petrie Rd. 8	43	J10
Phibsborough 7	35	J7
Phibsborough Av. 7	35	J7
Phibsborough Pl. 7	35	J7
Phibsborough Rd. 7	35	J7
Philipsburgh Av. 3	36	M6
Philipsburgh Ter. 3	36	M6
Philomena Ter. 4	45	N9
Phoenix Ct. 7	42	H8
Brodin Row		
Phoenix Manor 7	34	G7
Phoenix St. 7	43	J8
Phoenix St. 10	41	E9
Phoenix Ter., D.L.	58	Q14
Pig La. 1	36	L7
Pigeon Ho. Rd. 4	45	O9
Piles Bldgs. 8	43	K9
Golden La.		
Piles Ter. 2	44	L9
Sandwith St. Upper		
Pim St. 8	42	H9
Pimlico 8	43	J9
Pimlico Sq. 8	43	J9
The Coombe		
Pine Gro. 14	53	F16
Pine Haven, D.L.	58	Q14
Pine Hurst 7	34	G6
Pine Rd. 4	45	O9
Pinebrook Av. 5	25	O4
Pinebrook Cres. 5	25	O4
Pinebrook Av.		
Pinebrook Gro. 5	25	O4
Pinebrook Rd.		
Pinebrook Ri. 5	25	O4
Pinebrook Rd. 5	25	O4
Pines, The 5	26	P4
Pinewood Av. 11	23	J2
Pinewood Cres. 11	23	J2
Pinewood Dr. 11	23	J2
Pinewood Grn. 11	23	J2
Pinewood Gro. 11	23	J2
Pinewood Pk. 14	54	G16
Pinewood Vills. 11	23	J2
Pleasants La. 8	43	K10
Pleasants Pl. 8	43	K10
Pleasants St. 8	43	K10
Plunkett Grn. 11	21	F2
Plunkett Rd. 11	21	F2
Poddle Pk. 12	48	G13
Polo Rd. 8	33	F7
Poolbeg St. 2	44	L8
Poole St. 8	43	J9
Poplar Row 3	36	M6
Poplars, The, D.L.	60	T16
Port Side Ct. 3	36	M7
Portland Clo. 1	36	L7
Portland Pl. 1	35	K6
Portland Row 1	36	L7
Portland St. 8	42	H9
Portland St. N. 1	36	L7
Portmahon Dr. 8	42	G10
Portobello Bri. 6	49	K11

Portobello Harbour 8 49 K11
Portobello Pl. 8 49 K11
Portobello Rd. 8 49 J11
Portobello Sq. 8 49 J11
  Clanbrassil St. Upper
Potato Mkt. 7 43 J8
  Green St. Little
Powers Ct. 2 44 M10
  Warrington Pl.
Powers Sq. 8 43 J9
  John Dillon St.
Prebend St. 7 43 J8
Preston St. 1 44 L8
Price's La. 2 43 K8
Prices La. 6 49 K11
Priestfield Cotts. 8 42 H10
Priestfield Dr. 8 42 H10
  South Circular Rd.
Priestfield Ter. 8 42 H10
  South Circular Rd.
Primrose Av. 7 35 J7
Primrose Hill, D.L. 60 U16
Primrose St. 7 35 J7
Prince Arthur Ter. 6 49 K12
Prince of Wales Ter. 4 51 N11
Princes St. N. 1 43 K8
Princes St. S. 2 44 L9
Princeton 14 57 N15
Priory, The 7 33 F5
Priory Av., Stillorgan 58 Q15
Priory Dr., Stillorgan 58 P16
Priory E. 7 33 F5
Priory Gro., Stillorgan 58 P16
Priory Hall, D.L. 58 P16
Priory N. 7 33 F5
Priory Rd. 6 48 H12
Priory W. 7 33 F5
Proby Sq., D.L. 59 R16
Probys La. 1 43 K8
Promenade Rd. 1 37 O7
Prospect Av. 9 35 J5
Prospect Cem. 11 35 J5
Prospect La. 6 50 M13
Prospect Rd. 9 35 J6
Prospect Sq. 9 35 J5
Prospect Ter. 4 45 O10
  (Sandymount)
Prospect Way 9 35 J6
Protestant Row 2 43 K10
Prouds La. 2 43 K10
Prussia St. 7 34 H7
Purser Gdns. 6 49 K12
Pyro Vills. 8 42 H10

Q
Quarry Dr. 12 47 E13
Quarry Rd. (Cabra) 7 34 H6
Queen Maev Bri. 8 43 J8
Queen St. 7 43 J8
Queens Pk., D.L. 59 S16
Queens Rd., D.L. 61 V16
Quinns La. 2 44 L10

R
Rafters Av. 12 47 F11
Rafters La. 12 47 F11
Rafters Rd. 12 47 F11
Raglan La. 4 50 M11
Raglan Rd. 4 50 M11
Raheny Pk. 5 27 S4
Raheny Rd. 5 27 R3
Raheny Sta. 5 27 R4
Railway Av. 8 41 E10
  Tyrconnell Rd.
Railway Av. 40 D10
  (Inchicore)
Railway Av., Sutton 29 W2
Railway Cotts. 4 51 N11
  Serpentine Av.
Railway St. 1 44 L8
Railway Ter. 2 44 M9
  Grattan St.
Rainsford Av. 8 42 H9
Rainsford St. 8 42 H9
Raleigh Sq. 12 47 F11
Ramillies Rd. 10 40 C9
Ramleh Clo. 6 50 M13
Ramleh Pk. 6 50 M13

Ramleh Vills. 6 50 L13
Ranelagh Av. 6 50 L11
Ranelagh Rd. 6 49 K11
Raphoe Rd. 12 47 F11
Rath Row 2 44 L8
Rathdown Av. 6 54 H14
Rathdown Ct. 6 48 H13
Rathdown Cres. 6 54 H14
Rathdown Dr. 6 54 H14
Rathdown Pk. 6 54 H14
Rathdown Rd. 7 35 J7
Rathdown Sq. 7 34 H7
Rathdown Vills. 6 54 H14
Rathfarnham Bri. 14 54 H15
Rathfarnham Gate 14 54 H15
Rathfarnham Castle 14 54 H15
Rathfarnham Mill 14 54 H15
Rathfarnham Pk. 14 54 H14
Rathfarnham Rd. 14 54 H15
Rathfarnham Wd. 14 55 J15
Rathgar Av. 6 49 J12
Rathgar Pk. 6 49 J13
Rathgar Rd. 6 49 J13
Rathland Rd. 48 G13
  (Bothar Raiteann) 12
Rathlin Rd. 9 23 K4
Rathmines Av. 6 49 K12
Rathmines Castle 6 49 K12
Rathmines Rd. Lwr. 6 49 K12
Rathmines Rd. 49 K12
  Upper 6
Rathmore Pk. 5 27 S4
Rathvale Av. 5 26 Q2
Rathvale Dr. 5 26 Q2
Rathvale Gro. 5 26 Q2
  Rathvale Av.
Rathvale Pk. 5 26 Q2
Rathvilly Dr. 11 21 F4
Rathvilly Pk. 11 21 F3
Rathvilly Rd. 11 21 F3
Ratoath Av. 21 E3
  (Ascal Ratabhachta) 11
Ratoath Dr. 11 21 E3
Ratoath Rd. 7 34 G5
Ratoath Rd. 11 21 E3
Ratra Rd. 7 33 E6
Ravensdale Pk. 12 48 G13
Ravensdale Rd. 3 37 N7
Raymond St. 8 43 J10
Red Cow La. 7 43 J8
Redesdale Cres., 57 O16
  Stillorgan
Redesdale Rd., 57 O16
  Stillorgan
Redmonds Hill 2 43 K10
Redwood Ct. 14 55 K15
Redwood Gro., 58 Q15
  Blackrock
Reginald Sq. 8 43 J9
  Gray St.
Reginald St. 8 43 J9
Rehoboth Av. 8 42 H10
Rehoboth Pl. 8 42 H10
Reillys Av. 8 42 H10
  Dolphin's Barn St.
Reuben Av. 8 42 H10
Reuben St. 8 42 H10
Rialto Bri. 8 42 G10
Rialto Bldgs. 8 42 G10
Rialto Dr. 8 42 G10
Rialto St. 8 42 G10
Ribh Av. 5 26 Q4
Ribh Rd. 5 26 Q4
Richelieu Pk. 4 51 O12
Richmond Av., D.L. 60 T16
Richmond Av. N. 3 36 M6
Richmond Av. S. 6 50 L13
Richmond Cotts. 41 F9
  (Inchicore) 8
Richmond Ct. 6 56 L14
Richmond Cres. 1 36 L7
Richmond Est. 3 36 M6
Richmond Grn., D.L. 60 T16
Richmond Gro., D.L. 60 T16
Richmond Hill 6 49 K11
Richmond Hill, D.L. 60 T16
Richmond La. 1 36 L7
  Russell St.
Richmond Ms. 6 49 K11

Richmond Par. 1 36 L7
Richmond Pk., D.L. 60 T16
Richmond Pl. 6 49 K11
Richmond Pl. S. 2 49 K11
  Richmond St. S.
Richmond Rd. 3 36 L5
Richmond Row 8 49 K11
Richmond Row S. 2 43 K10
  Richmond St. S.
Richmond St. N. 1 36 L7
Richmond St. S. 2 43 K10
Richmonds Cotts. 1 36 L7
Richview Masonic 50 M13
  Sch. 14
Richview Pk. 6 50 L13
Ring St. 8 40 D10
Ring Ter. 8 41 E10
Ringsend Bri. 4 45 N9
Ringsend Pk. 4 45 N9
Ringsend Rd. 4 44 M9
Rise, The 23 K4
  (Drumcondra) 9
Rise, The, Mount 58 P15
  Merrion
River Gdns. 9 35 K5
River Rd., 20 D3
  Castleknock
Riversdale Av. 6 55 J14
Riversdale Gro. 6 48 G13
Riverside Cotts. 6 54 G15
Riverside Dr. 14 55 J15
Riverside Wk. 4 50 M13
Riverston Abbey 7 33 F5
Riverview Ct., 40 C8
  Chapelizod
Road No. 1 1 45 O8
Road No. 2 1 45 O8
Road No. 3 1 45 O8
Robert Emmet Bri. 6 49 J11
Robert Pl. 3 36 L6
  Clonliffe Rd.
Robert St. 3 36 L6
  Clonliffe Rd.
Robert St. 8 42 H9
Robinsons Ct. 8 43 J9
Rock Hill, D.L. 59 R15
Rock Rd., 63 P13
  Booterstown
Rockfield Av. 12 53 E14
Rockfield Dr. 12 47 F13
Rockford Pk., D.L. 59 S16
Rockville Cres., D.L. 59 S16
Rockville Dr., D.L. 59 S16
Rockville Pk., D.L. 59 S16
Rockville Rd., D.L. 59 S16
Roebuck Av., 58 P15
  Stillorgan
Roebuck Castle 14 57 N14
Roebuck Downs 14 56 M15
Roebuck Dr. 12 47 E13
Roebuck Hall 14 57 N15
Roebuck Rd. 14 56 M14
Roger's La. 2 44 L10
Roncalli Rd., 28 U3
  Kilbarrack
Roosevelt Cotts. 7 33 F6
Rope Wk. Pl. 4 45 N9
Rory O'Connor Pk., 60 T17
  D.L.
Rory O'More Bri. 8 42 H8
Rosapenna Dr. 5 27 S2
Rosary Gdns. E., D.L. 61 U16
Rosary Gdns. W., 60 U16
  D.L.
Rosary Rd. 8 42 H10
Rosary Ter. 4 45 N9
Rosbeg Ct., Kilbarrack 29 U3
Rose Glen Av. 5 28 T3
Rose Glen Rd. 5 27 S3
Rose Pk., D.L. 60 T17
Rosemount 56 M15
  (Dundrum Rd.) 14
Rosemount 56 M14
  (Roebuck Rd.) 14
Rosemount Av. 5 26 P4
Rosemount Ct., D.L. 58 P14
Rosemount Pk. 14 56 M15
Rosemount Rd. 7 35 J7
Rosemount Ter., 58 P14
  Booterstown

Rosevale Ct. 5 26
  Brookwood Glen
Rosevale Mans. 5 26
Rosmeen Gdns., D.L. 61
Rosmeen Pk., D.L. 61
Ross Rd. 8 43
Ross St. 7 34
Rossmore Av. 12 53
Rossmore Clo. 12 53
Rossmore Cres. 12 53
Rossmore Dr. 12 53
Rossmore Gro. 12 53
Rossmore Lawn 12 53
Rossmore Pk. 12 53
Rossmore Rd. 12 53
Rostrevor Rd. 6 55
Rostrevor Ter. 6 55
Rothe Abbey 8 42
Rotunda Hosp. 1 43
Rowan Hall 6 50
  Prospect La.
Rowan Pk. Av., 59
  Stillorgan
Rowanbyrn Est., D.L. 59
Royal Canal Bk. 7 35
Royal Canal Ter. 7 35
  Royal Hosp. 8 42
Royal Marine Rd., D.L. 61
Royal Ter. 3 36
  Inverness Rd.
Royal Ter. E., D.L. 61
Royal Ter. La., D.L. 61
Royal Ter. N., D.L. 61
Royal Ter. W., D.L. 61
Royal Veterinary 45
  Coll. 4
Royal Victoria Eye & 44
  Ear Hosp. 2
Royse Rd. 7 35
Royston 12 49
Rugby Rd. 6 49
Rugby Vills. 6 49
  Rugby Rd.
Rushbrook Av., 53
  Tallaght
Rushbrook Ct., 53
  Tallaght
Rushbrook Dr., 53
  Tallaght
Rushbrook Gro., 53
  Tallaght
Rushbrook Pk., 53
  Tallaght
Rushbrook Vw., 52
  Tallaght
Rushbrook Way, 53
  Tallaght
Russell Av. 3 36
Russell Av. E. 3 44
Russell St. 1 36
Rutland Av. 12 48
Rutland Gro. 12 48
Rutland Pl. 3 36
  Clontarf Rd.
Rutland Pl. N. 1 36
Rutland Pl. W. 1 35
Rutland St. Lwr. 1 36
Rutledges Ter. 8 42
Ryders Row 1 43
  Parnell St.

S
Sackville Av. 3 36
Sackville Gdns. 3 36
Sackville La. 1 43
  O'Connell St. Lwr.
St. Agnes Pk. 12 47
St. Agnes Rd. 12 47
St. Aidan's Dr. 14 57
St. Aidan's Pk. 3 37
St. Aidan's Pk. Av. 3 37
St. Aidan's Pk. Rd. 3 37
St. Alban's Pk. 4 51
St. Alban's Rd. 8 43
St. Alphonsus Av. 9 35
St. Alphonsus Rd. 9 35
St. Andeons Ter. 8 4
  Cook St.

Name	Pg	Grid
ndrew's La. 2	43	K9
nity St.		
ndrew's St. 2	43	K9
nne's 12	48	G13
nne's Av. 5	27	R4
nne's City	50	L11
sp. 6		
nne's Dr. 5	27	R4
nne's Rd. 8	48	H11
nne's Rd. N. 9	35	K6
nne's Sq., D.L.	59	R15
nne's Ter. 5	27	R4
nthony's Cres. 2	46	D13
nthony's Pl. 1	35	K7
nthony's Rd. 8	42	G10
ongus Cres.,	52	C15
laght		
ongus Gro.,	52	C15
laght		
ongus Lawn,	52	C15
laght		
ongus Rd.,	52	C15
laght		
ssam's Av. 5	27	S4
ssam's Dr. 5	27	S4
ssam's Pk. 5	27	S4
ssam's Rd. E. 5	27	S4
ssam's Rd. W. 5	27	S4
ttracta Rd. 7	34	H6
udoens Ter. 8	43	J9
ugustine St. 8	43	J9
rnabas Gdns. 3	36	M7
endan's Av. 5	26	P3
endan's Cotts. 4	45	N9
endan's Cres. 12	54	D14
endan's Dr. 5	26	P3
endan's Hosp. 7	34	H7
endan's Pk. 5	26	Q3
endan's Ter. 5	26	P2
endan's Ter.,	61	U16
rary Rd.		
ricin's Hosp. 7	42	H8
ricin's Pk. 7	42	H8
ridget's Av. 3	36	M7
ridget's Av. 12	46	D13
ridget's Ct. 5	26	P4
Brigid's Dr.		
rigids Cres. 5	26	P4
rigids Dr. 5	26	P4
rigids Flats 14	50	M13
rigids Gdns. 1	44	M8
rigids Grn. 5	26	P4
rigids Gro. 5	26	P4
rigids Lawn 5	26	P4
rigid's Rd. 5	26	P4
rigid's Rd. Lwr. 9	35	K6
rigid's Rd.	35	K6
per 9		
roc's Cotts. 4	50	M12
anice's Pk. 11	23	J3
anice's Rd. 11	23	J3
atherine's Av. 8	42	H10
atherine's La.	43	J9
8		
atherine's Pk.,	61	V17
lare's Av. 6	49	J11
rolds Cross Rd.		
lare's Home 9	23	J4
lare's Ter. 6	49	J11
unt Drummond Av.		
lement's Rd. 9	35	K6
olumbanus Av.	56	L14
olumbanus Pl.	56	L14
olumbanus Rd.	56	L14
olumba's Rd. 12	46	D13
olumba's Rd.	35	K6
r. 9		
olumba's Rd.	35	K6
per 9		
onleith's Rd. 12	46	D13
avids	25	O4
avids Pk. 5	25	O4
avid's Ter. 7	34	G7
ackhorse Av.		
St. David's Ter.	23	K4
(Glasnevin) 9		
St. Davids Wd. 5	25	O4
St. Declan Rd. 3	36	M5
St. Declan Ter. 3	37	N5
St. Donagh's Cres. 5	27	S2
St. Donagh's Pk. 5	28	T2
St. Donagh's Rd. 5	27	S2
St. Eithne Rd. 7	34	H6
St. Elizabeth's Ct. 7	34	H7
North Circular Rd.		
St. Enda's Dr. 14	54	H16
St. Enda's Rd. 6	49	J13
St. Finbar's Clo. 12	52	D14
St. Finbar's Rd. 7	34	G5
St. Fintan Rd. 7	34	H6
St. Fintan Ter. 7	34	H6
St. Fintan's Cres.	30	Y4
Howth		
St. Fintan's Gro.,	30	Y4
Howth		
St. Fintan's Pk.,	30	Y4
Howth		
St. Fintan's Pk.,	60	S17
Stillorgan		
St. Fintan's Rd.,	30	Y4
Howth		
St. Gabriels Ct. 3	39	R6
St. Gabriel's Rd. 3	39	R6
St. Gall Gdns. N. 14	56	L14
St. Gall Gdns. S. 14	56	L14
St. George's Av. 3	36	L6
St. Gerard's Rd. 12	47	E13
St. Helena's Dr. 11	22	G4
St. Helena's Rd. 11	21	F4
St. Helens, D.L.	61	W17
St. Helen's Rd., D.L.	58	P14
St. Helens Wd., D.L.	58	P15
St. Ignatius Av. 7	35	K6
St. Ignatius Rd. 7	35	K6
St. Ita's Rd. 9	35	K5
St. James's Av. 3	36	L6
St. James's Av. 8	42	H9
Tyrconnell Rd.		
St. James's Rd. 12	46	D13
St. James's Ter. 8	42	H10
St. James's Wk. 8	42	G10
St. Jarlath Rd. 7	34	H6
St. Johns 4	51	O12
St. John's Av. 8	43	J9
John St. S.		
St. Johns Ct. 3	37	O5
St. Johns Ct. 5	25	O2
St. John's Pk., D.L.	60	U16
St. John's Rd. E. 4	51	O11
St. John's Rd. W. 8	41	F9
St. John's St. 8	43	J10
Black Pitts		
St. Johns Wd. 3	38	P6
St. Joseph's Av. 3	36	L6
St. Joseph's Av. 9	35	K6
St. Joseph's	35	K7
Childrens Hosp. 1		
St. Joseph's	48	H13
Convent 6		
St. Josephs Ct. 7	34	H7
St. Josephs Gro. 14	56	M16
St. Joseph's Par. 7	35	K7
St. Joseph's Pl. 7	35	K7
Dorset St. Upper		
St. Joseph's Rd. 7	34	H7
St. Joseph's Rd. 12	46	D13
St. Joseph's Sq. 3	38	Q7
Vernon Av.		
St. Joseph's St. 7	35	K7
Synnott Pl.		
St. Joseph's Ter. 1	36	L7
North Circular Rd.		
St. Joseph's Ter. 3	36	M6
St. Kevins Ct. 6	49	K13
St. Kevins Gdns. 6	49	K13
St. Kevin's Par. 8	43	J10
St. Kevins Pk.	49	K13
(Rathgar) 6		
St. Kevin's Rd. 8	49	J11
St. Killian's Av. 12	52	D14
St. Laurence Gro. 10	40	C9
St. Laurence Rd.,	40	C9
Chapelizod		
St. Laurence St. N. 1	44	M8
Sheriff St. Lwr.		
St. Laurence's	44	M8
Mans. 1		
St. Laurences Pk.,	58	P16
Stillorgan		
St. Lawrence Pl. 1	44	L8
Sheriff St. Lwr.		
St. Lawrence Rd.	37	O6
(Clontarf) 3		
St. Lawrence Rd.,	31	AA3
Howth		
St. Lawrence St. 1	44	L8
Sheriff St. Lwr.		
St. Lawrence Ter.,	31	BB3
Howth		
St. Lawrences Ct. 3	37	O6
St. Luke's Cres. 14	56	L14
St. Luke's Hosp. 6	55	K14
St. Magdalene Ter. 4	45	N9
St. Malachy's Dr. 12	46	D13
St. Malachy's Rd. 9	35	K5
St. Margaret's Av. 5	28	T3
St. Margaret's Av. N. 1	36	L7
North Circular Rd.		
St. Margaret's Ter. 8	42	G13
St. Martin's Dr. 12	48	G13
St. Martin's Pk. 12	48	H12
St. Mary's Av.	54	H15
(Rathfarnham) 14		
St. Mary's Av. N. 7	35	K7
St. Mary's Av. W. 10	41	E9
St. Mary's Coll. 4	50	M11
St. Mary's Coll. 6	49	K11
St. Mary's Coll. 9	36	M5
St. Mary's Cres. 12	47	E12
St. Mary's Dr. 12	47	E11
St. Mary's Home for	63	P13
Blind 4		
St. Mary's Hosp.,	40	D8
Chapelizod		
St. Mary's La. 4	44	M10
St. Mary's	20	D2
Orthopaedic Hosp. 11		
St. Mary's Pk. 11	21	E3
St. Mary's Pk. 12	47	E12
St. Mary's Pl. 7	35	K7
St. Mary's Rd.,	31	BB3
Howth		
Main St.		
St. Mary's Rd. N. 3	36	M7
St. Mary's Rd. S. 4	44	M10
St. Mary's St., D.L.	60	U16
St. Mary's Ter. 7	35	K7
St. Mel's Av. 12	52	D14
St. Michael's Hill 8	43	J9
St. Michael's Hosp.,	61	V16
D.L.		
St. Michael's La. 8	43	J9
High St.		
St. Michael's Rd. 9	35	K5
St. Michael's Ter. 8	43	J10
St. Michan's St. 7	43	J8
St. Mobhi Boithirin 9	23	K4
St. Mobhi Ct. 9	23	K4
St. Mobhi Dr. 9	35	K5
St. Mobhi Gro. 9	35	K5
St. Mobhi Rd. 9	35	K5
St. Mobhis Bri. 9	35	K5
St. Nessan's Ter.,	31	BB3
Howth		
Tuckett's La.		
St. Nicholas Pl. 8	43	J9
St. Pappin Grn. 11	23	J3
St. Pappin Rd. 11	23	J3
St. Patrick Av. 3	36	M7
North Strand Rd.		
St. Patrick's	43	J9
Cathedral 8		
St. Patrick's Clo., D.L.	60	T17
St. Patrick's Cotts. 14	54	H16
St. Patrick's Cres.	60	T17
D.L.		
St. Patrick's Hosp. 8	42	G9
St. Patrick's Par. 9	35	K6
St. Patrick's Rd. 9	35	K6
St. Patrick's Rd. 12	46	D13
St. Patrick's Ter. 1	36	L7
Russell St.		
St. Patrick's Ter. 3	36	M7
North Strand Rd.		
St. Patrick's Ter. 8	41	E9
St. Patricks Ter., D.L.	60	U17
St. Patrick's Training	36	L5
Coll. 9		
St. Patrick's Vills. 4	45	N9
St. Paul St. 7	43	J8
St. Paul's Hosp. 9	25	N2
St. Paul's Ter., D.L.	61	W17
St. Peters Av. 7	35	J7
St. Peters Clo. 7	35	J7
St. Peter's Cres. 12	47	E13
St. Peter's Dr. 12	47	E13
St. Peter's Rd. 7	35	J6
St. Peter's Rd. 12	46	D13
St. Peter's Ter., D.L.	61	W17
St. Peter's Ter.,	31	AA3
Howth		
St. Philomena's Rd. 11	35	J6
St. Stephen's Grn.	44	L10
E. 2		
St. Stephen's Grn.	43	K9
N. 2		
St. Stephen's Grn.	43	K10
Pk. 2		
St. Stephen's Grn.	43	K10
S. 2		
St. Stephen's Grn.	43	K10
W. 2		
St. Teresa's Pl. 9	35	J5
Prospect Av.		
St. Teresa's Rd. 9	35	J5
St. Teresa's Rd.	47	F13
(Crumlin) 12		
St. Theresa Gdns. 8	42	H10
St. Thomas' Rd.	43	J10
(Tenter Flds.) 8		
St. Thomas' Rd.,	57	O15
Stillorgan		
St. Thomas's Av. 7	43	J8
Constitution Hill		
St. Thomas's Mead,	58	P15
Stillorgan		
St. Vincent St.	43	J10
(Tenter Flds.) 8		
St. Vincent St. N. 7	35	J7
St. Vincent St. W. 8	41	E9
St. Vincent's Home 7	33	E5
St. Vincent's Hosp. 2	44	L10
St. Vincent's Pk., D.L.	59	S15
Salamanca 14	57	N15
Sallymount Av. 6	50	L11
Sallymount Gdns. 6	50	L11
Sally's Bri. 8	48	H11
Salthill &	60	T15
Monkstown Sta., D.L.		
Salzburg 14	57	N15
Sampsons La. 1	43	K8
Sandford Av.	50	M12
(Donnybrook) 4		
Sandford Av. 8	42	H10
Sandford Clo. 6	50	L12
Sandford Gdns. 8	50	M12
Sandford Gdns. 8	42	H10
Donore Av.		
Sandford Rd. 6	50	L12
Sandford Ter. 6	50	L12
Sandon Cove 3	38	P6
Sandwith Pl. 2	44	L9
Sandwith St. Lwr. 2	44	L9
Sandwith St. Upper 2	44	L9
Sandycove Av. N.,	61	W16
D.L.		
Sandycove Av. W.,	61	W17
D.L.		
Sandycove Glastule	61	V17
Sta., D.L.		
Sandycove Point,	61	W16
D.L.		
Sandycove Rd., D.L.	61	W17
Sandyhill Av. 11	23	J2
Sandymount Av. 4	51	N11
Sandymount Castle	51	O11
Dr. 4		
Sandymount Castle	51	O11
Rd. 4		
Sandymount Grn. 4	45	O10

77

Entry	Page	Grid
Sandymount Rd. 4	45	O10
Sandymount Sta. 4	51	O11
Sans Souci Pk., D.L.	58	P14
Santa Sabina Manor, Howth	30	Y3
Sarah Pl. 8	41	F8
Sarsfield Quay 7	42	H8
Sarsfield Rd. 10	40	D9
Sarsfield St. 7	35	J7
Sarto Lawn, Kilbarrack	28	U2
Sarto Pk., Kilbarrack	28	U3
Sarto Ri., Sutton	28	U3
Sarto Rd., Kilbarrack	28	U3
Saul Rd. 12	48	G11
School Av. 5	26	P4
School Ho. La. W. 8	43	J9
School St. 8	42	H9
Schoolhouse La. 2	44	L9
Sea Vw. Ter. 4	51	N12
Seabank Ct., D.L.	61	W17
Seabury 4	63	P12
Seacliff Av., Baldoyle	29	V2
Seacliff Dr., Baldoyle	29	U2
Seacourt 3	39	R6
Seafield Av. 3	38	Q6
Seafield Av., Stillorgan	60	T16
Seafield Clo., Stillorgan	57	O14
Seafield Ct., Howth	29	W2
Seafield Cres., Stillorgan	58	P14
Seafield Down 3	39	R6
Seafield Dr., Booterstown	58	P14
Seafield Gro. 3	39	R6
Seafield Pk., Booterstown	58	P14
Seafield Rd., Stillorgan	57	O14
Seafield Rd. E. 3	38	Q6
Seafield Rd. W. 3	38	P6
Seafort Av. 4	45	O10
Seafort Cotts. 4 (Seafort Av.)	45	O10
Seafort Gdns. 4	45	O10
Seafort Vills. 4 (Seafort Av.)	45	O10
Seagrange Av., Baldoyle	28	U2
Seagrange Dr., Baldoyle	29	V2
Seagrange Rd., Baldoyle	29	U2
Sean Heuston Bri. 8	42	H8
Sean McDermott St. Lwr. 1	44	L8
Sean McDermott St. Upper 1	43	K8
Sean More Rd. 4	45	O10
Sean O'Casey La. 1	36	L7
Seapark Dr. 3	38	Q6
Seapark Rd. 3	38	Q6
Seapoint Av., D.L.	59	S15
Seaview Av. E. 3	36	M7
Seaview Av. N. 3	37	O6
Seaview Ter., Howth	31	BB3
Second Av. 1	44	M8
Second Av. (Rialto) 8	42	G10
Selskar Ter. 6	49	K11
Serpentine Av. 4	45	N10
Serpentine Pk. 4	45	N10
Serpentine Rd. 4	45	N10
Serpentine Ter. 4	51	N11
Seven Oaks 9	24	L4
Seventh Av. 8	42	G10
Seville Pl. 1	44	M8
Seville Ter. 1	36	M7
Shamrock Cotts. 1 (Shamrock Pl.)	36	M7
Shamrock Pl. 1	36	M7
Shamrock St. 7 (Primrose St.)	35	J7
Shamrock Ter. 1	36	M7
Shamrock Vills. 6	49	J12
Shanard Av. 9	23	K3
Shanard Rd. 9	23	K2
Shanboley Rd. 9	24	M2
Shandon Cres. 7	35	J6
Shandon Dr. 7	35	J6
Shandon Gdns. 7	34	H6
Shandon Pk. 7	35	J6
Shandon Pk., D.L.	59	S15
Shandon Rd. 7	35	J6
Shangan Av. 9	24	L2
Shangan Gdns. 9	24	L2
Shangan Grn. 9	24	L2
Shangan Pk. 9	24	L2
Shangan Rd. 9	23	K2
Shangangh Rd. 9	35	K6
Shanglas Rd. 9	24	M3
Shanid Rd. 6	48	H13
Shanliss Av. 9	24	L2
Shanliss Dr. 9	24	L2
Shanliss Gro. 9	24	L2
Shanliss Pk. 9	24	L2
Shanliss Rd. 9	23	K2
Shanliss Wk. 9	24	L2
Shanliss Way 9	24	L2
Shannon Ter. 8	42	G9
Shanowen Av. 9	24	L3
Shanowen Cres. 9	24	L3
Shanowen Dr. 9	24	L3
Shanowen Gro. 9	23	K2
Shanowen Pk. 9	23	K3
Shanowen Rd. 9	24	L3
Shanrath Rd. 9	24	M3
Shantalla Av. 9	24	M3
Shantalla Dr. 9	24	M3
Shantalla Pk. 9	24	M3
Shantalla Rd. 9	24	M3
Shanvarna Rd. 9	24	M3
Shaw St. 2	44	L9
Shaws La. 4	45	N10
Shelbourne Av. 4	45	N10
Shelbourne La. 4	51	N11
Shelbourne Pk. Greyhound Race Course 4	45	N9
Shelbourne Rd. 4	45	N10
Shellysbanks Rd. 4	62	P10
Shelmalier Rd. 3	36	M7
Shelmartin Av. 3	36	M6
Shelmartin Ter. 3	36	M6
Shelton Dr. 12	47	F13
Shelton Gdns. 12	47	F13
Shelton Gro. 12	47	F13
Shelton Pk. 12	47	F13
Sheriff St. Lwr. 1	44	L8
Sheriff St. Upper 1	44	M8
Sherkin Gdns. 9	24	L4
Sherrard Av. 1	35	K7
Sherrard St. Lwr. 1	35	K7
Sherrard St. Upper 1	35	K7
Shielmartin Dr., Howth	30	Y4
Shielmartin Pk., Howth	30	Y5
Shielmartin Rd., Howth	30	Y4
Ship St. Great 8	43	K9
Ship St. Little 8	43	K9
Shrewsbury 4	51	O11
Shrewsbury Pk. 4	51	O11
Shrewsbury Rd. 4	51	N12
Sibthorpe La. 6	50	L11
Sigurd Rd. 7	42	H8
Silchester Ct., D.L.	61	V17
Silchester Cres., D.L.	61	V17
Silchester Pk., D.L.	61	V17
Silchester Rd., D.L.	61	V17
Silloge Av. 11	23	J2
Silloge Gdns. 11	23	K2
Silloge Rd. 11	23	K2
Silver Birches 14	56	M16
Silverwood Dr. 6 (Templeville Dr.)	53	F15
Silverwood Rd. 14	54	G16
Silverwood Rd. 14	54	G16
Simmonscourt (Donnybrook)	50	M12
Simmonscourt Av. 4	51	N12
Simmonscourt Castle 4	51	N12
Simmonscourt Rd. 4	51	N12
Simmonscourt Ter. 4	51	N12
Simonscourt Sq. 4	51	N11
Simonscourt Vw. 4	51	N11
Sion Hill, D.L.	58	Q14
Sion Hill Av. 6	48	H12
Sion Hill Ct. 9	36	M5
Sion Hill Rd. 9	24	M4
Sir John Rogersons Quay 2	44	M8
Sir Patrick Duns Hosp. 2	44	M9
Sitric Rd. 7	42	H8
Sixth Av. 8	42	G10
Skellys La. 5	25	N3
Skippers All. 8	43	J9
Skreen Rd. 7	33	F6
Slade Row 7	42	H8
Slademore Av. 5	26	Q2
Slademore Clo. 5	27	R2
Slademore Ct. 5	26	Q2
Slademore Dr. 5	27	R2
Slane Rd. 12	48	G11
Slaney Rd. 11	34	H5
Slemish Rd. 7	33	F6
Slieve Rua Dr., Stillorgan	57	O16
Slievebloom Pk. 12	47	E11
Slievebloom Rd. 12	47	E11
Slievemore Rd. 12	47	F11
Slievenamon Rd. 12	42	G10
Sloperton, D.L.	60	U16
Slopes, The, D.L.	60	U16
Smithfield 7	43	J8
Smiths Vills., D.L.	60	U16
Somerset St. 4	45	N9
Somerville Av. 12	47	E12
Somerville Grn. 12	47	E12
Somerville Pk. 12	47	E12
Sommerville 14	56	M15
Sorbonne 14	57	N15
South Av., Stillorgan	58	P16
South Bk. Rd. 4	45	O9
South Circular Rd. 8	41	F8
South Docks Rd. 4	45	N9
South Great Georges St. 2	43	K9
South Hill 6	50	L13
South Hill, Howth	30	Y4
South Hill Av., D.L.	58	P15
South Hill Pk., D.L.	58	P15
South Lotts Rd. 4	45	N10
South Rd. No. 4 1 (Alexandra Rd.)	62	P8
Southdene, D.L.	60	T16
Southern Cross Av. 8	41	F9
Southwood, D.L.	58	Q15
Spa Rd. (Kilmainham) 8	41	E9
Spa Rd. (Phoenix Pk.) 8	33	F7
Spafield Ter. 4	51	N11
Spencer Av. 1	44	M8
Spencer Dock 1 (Guild St.)	44	M8
Spencer St. 8 (South Circular Rd.)	43	J10
Spencer St. N. 3	36	M7
Spencer Vills., D.L.	61	W17
Sperrin Rd. 12	47	E11
Spire Vw. Ct. 6	49	J12
Spire Vw. La. 6	49	J12
Spitalfields 8	43	J9
Spring Gdn. La. 2	44	L9
Spring Gdn. St. 3	36	M7
Springdale Rd. 5	26	Q3
Springfield 7	33	F6
Springfield Av. 6	54	G15
Springfield Cres. 6	54	G15
Springfield Dr. 6	54	G15
Springfield Pk. 6	54	G15
Springfield Rd. 6	54	G15
Springhill Pk., Stillorgan	60	S17
Square, The 4	45	N9
Square, The 6	48	H12
Stable La. 2 (Harcourt St.)	43	K10
Stable La. 4 (Londonbridge Rd.)	45	N10
Stables, The, D.L.	58	P14
Stamer St. 8	43	K10
Stanford Grn. 12	47	E12
Stanhope St. 7	43	J8
Stannaway Av. 12	47	F12
Stannaway Dr. 12	48	G12
Stannaway Rd. 12	48	G12
Station Rd. 5	27	
Station Rd., Sutton	29	
Steeples, The 10	40	
Steevens Hosp. 8	42	
Steevens La. 8	42	
Stella Av. 9	23	
Stephen St. 2	43	
Stephen St. Upper 8	43	
Stephens La. 2	44	M
Stephens Pl. 2 (Stephens La.)	44	M
Stephens Rd. 8	41	
Stiles Ct., The 3 (The Stiles Rd.)	37	
Stiles Rd., The 3	37	
Stillorgan Bypass, Stillorgan	58	
Stillorgan Pk., Stillorgan	58	
Stillorgan Pk. Av., Stillorgan	58	
Stillorgan Rd. 4	51	
Stillorgan Rd., Stillorgan	58	
Stirling Pk. 14	55	
Stirrup La. 7 (Beresford St.)	43	
Stonepark Abbey 14	55	
Stonepark Ct. 14	55	
Stonepark Dr. 14	55	
Stonepark Grn. 14	55	
Stoneview Pl., D.L.	61	
Stoney Rd. 3 (East Wall Rd.)	36	
Stoney Rd. (Dundrum) 14	56	M
Stoneybatter 7	42	
Store St. 1	44	
Stormanstown Rd. 11	23	
Stradbrook, D.L.	59	
Stradbrook Clo., Stillorgan	60	
Stradbrook Gdns., D.L. (Stradbrook Rd.)	59	
Stradbrook Hill, Stillorgan	60	
Stradbrook Lawn, D.L.	59	
Stradbrook Pk., D.L.	59	
Stradbrook Rd., D.L.	59	
Strand Rd. (Sandymount) 4	51	
Strand Rd., Howth	30	
Strand St. 4	45	
Strand St. Great 1	43	
Strand St. Little 7	43	
Strandville Av. E. 3	37	
Strandville Av. N. 3	36	
Strandville Ho. 3	37	
Strangford Gdns. 3	36	
Strangford Rd. 3	36	
Streamville Rd. 5	27	
Suffolk St. 2	43	
Suir Rd. 8	41	
Sullivan St. 7	42	
Summer Pl. 1	36	
Summer St. N. 1	36	
Summer St. S. 8	42	
Summerhill 1	36	
Summerhill Par. 1	36	
Summerhill Par., D.L.	61	
Summerhill Pl. 1	36	
Summerhill Rd., D.L.	61	
Summerville 3	38	
Summerville Pk. 6	49	
Sunbury Gdns. 6	49	
Sundrive Pk. 12	48	
Sundrive Rd. 12	48	
Sunnyside Ms. 3	38	
Susan Rd. 8	43	
Susanville Rd. 3	36	
Sussex Rd. 4	50	
Sussex St., D.L.	61	
Sussex Ter. Lwr. 4 (Mespil Rd.)	44	
Sussex Ter. Upper 4 (Leeson St. Upper)	50	
Sutton Ct., Kilbarrack	29	

Name	Page	Grid
utton Downs, Kilbarrack	29	V3
utton Gro., Kilbarrack	29	V2
utton Lawns, Sutton	29	V2
utton Sta., Sutton	29	W2
wan Pl. 4	50	M11
Morehampton Rd.		
wan Yd. 2	43	K9
Harry St.		
wans Nest Av. 5	28	T3
wans Nest Ct. 5	28	T3
wans Nest Rd. 5	27	S2
wanville Pl. 6	49	K12
wanward Ct. 12	48	H11
weeneys Ter. 8	43	J10
Mill St.		
weetmans Av., D.L.	59	R15
weetmont Av. 14	56	L16
weetmont Dr. 14	56	L16
weetmont Pk. 14	56	L16
wifts All. 8	43	J9
wifts Row 7	43	J9
Ormond Quay Upper		
willy Rd. 7	34	G6
words Rd. 9	24	L4
words St. 7	42	H8
ybil Hill Av. 5	26	Q4
ybil Hill Rd. 5	26	Q4
ycamore Cres., Stillorgan	58	P15
ycamore Pk. 11	22	H2
ycamore Rd. 11	22	H2
(Finglas) 11		
ycamore Rd., Mount Merrion	58	P15
ycamore St. 2	43	K9
ydenham Ms., D.L.	61	V16
ydenham Rd.	51	N11
(Sandymount) 4		
ydenham Rd.	56	M16
(Dundrum) 14		
ydenham Vills. 14	56	M16
ydney Av. 4	59	R15
ydney Par. Av. 4	59	R15
ydney Par. Sta. 4	51	O12
ydney Ter., D.L.	59	R15
ykes La. 6	49	J13
ynge La. 8	43	K10
ynge St. 8	43	K10
ynnott Pl. 7	35	K7
ynnott Row 7	35	K7

T

Name	Page	Grid
albot La. 1	44	L8
Talbot St.		
albot La., Stillorgan	58	Q16
albot Pl. 1	44	L8
lbot St. 1	44	L8
allaght Rd., Tallaght	52	C16
aney Av. 14	56	M16
aney Ct. 14	56	M16
aney Cres. 14	56	M16
aney Dr. 14	56	M16
aney Gro. 14	57	N16
aney Lawn 14	56	M16
aney Manor 14	56	M16
aney Pk. 14	56	M16
aney Ri. 14	56	M16
aney Rd. 14	56	M16
ra Hill Cres. 14	54	H16
ra Hill Gro. 14	54	H16
ra Hill Rd. 14	54	H16
ra Lawn 5	27	S2
ra St. 2	44	L8
ra St. Sta. 2	44	L8
ylors La. 8	42	H9
mple Bar 2	43	K9
mple Cotts. 7	35	J7
mple Ct. 7	42	H8
mple Cres., D.L.	59	S15
mple Gdns. 6	43	K9
mple Hill, D.L.	59	S15
mple La. N. 1	35	K7
mple La. S. 2	43	K9
mple Manor Av. 12	52	D14
mple Manor Clo. 12	52	D14
Temple Manor Ct. 12	52	D14
Temple Manor Dr. 12	52	D14
Temple Manor Gro. 12	52	D14
Temple Manor Way 12	52	D14
Temple Pk. 6	50	L13
Temple Pk. Av., D.L.	59	S15
Temple Pl. 6	50	L11
Temple Rd. 6	49	K13
Temple Rd., D.L.	59	R15
Temple Sq. 6	49	K13
Temple St. N. 1	35	K7
Temple St. W. 7	42	H8
Temple Vills. 6	49	K12
Palmerston Rd.		
Templemore Av. 6	49	K13
Templeogue Rd. 6	54	G15
Templeogue Wd. 12	53	F15
Templeville Av. 6	53	F15
Templeville Dr. 6	53	F15
Templeville Pk. 6	54	G15
Templeville Rd. 6	53	F14
Templeville Rd. 12	53	F14
Terenure Coll. 6	54	G14
Terenure Pk. 6	48	H13
Terenure Pl. 6	48	H13
Terenure Rd. E. 6	48	H13
Terenure Rd. N. 6	48	H13
Terenure Rd. W. 6	48	G13
Terminal Rd. N. 1	62	Q8
Thatch Rd., The 9	24	M4
Third Av. 1	44	M8
Third Av. 8	42	H10
Dolphin's Barn		
Third Av. (Rialto) 8	42	G10
Thomas Ct. 8	43	J9
Thomas Davis St. S. 8	43	J9
Thomas Davis St. W. 8	41	E10
Thomas La. 1	43	K8
Thomas St. E. 4	45	N9
Thomas St. W. 8	42	H9
Thomond Rd. 10	40	C9
Thor Pl. 7	42	H8
Thormanby Lawns, Howth	31	BB3
Thormanby Rd., Howth	31	BB3
Thormanby Wds., Howth	31	BB4
Thorncastle St. 4	45	N9
Thorncliffe Pk. 14	55	K14
Elm Mt. Rd.		
Thorndale Av. 5	25	O4
Thorndale Ct. 9	24	M4
Thorndale Cres. 5	25	O4
Elm Mt. Rd.		
Thorndale Dr. 5	25	O4
Thorndale Gro. 5	25	O4
Thorndale Lawn 5	25	O4
Elm Mt. Rd.		
Thorndale Pk. 5	25	O4
Elm Mt. Rd.		
Thornhill Rd., Stillorgan	57	O16
Thornville Av. 5	28	T3
Thornville Dr. 5	28	T3
Thornville Pk. 5	28	T3
Thornville Rd. 5	28	T3
Three Rock Clo. 12	52	C14
Kilmashogue Gro.		
Thundercat All. 7	43	J8
Smithfield		
Tibradden Clo. 12	52	C14
Tibradden Dr.		
Tibradden Dr. 12	52	C14
Tibradden Gro. 12	52	C14
Tibradden Dr.		
Timber Quay 1	45	O8
Tivoli Av. 6	49	J12
Tivoli Clo., D.L.	60	U17
Tivoli Rd., D.L.	60	U16
Tivoli Ter. E., D.L.	61	U16
Tivoli Ter. N., D.L.	60	U16
Tivoli Ter. S., D.L.	60	U16
Tolka Cotts. 11	22	H4
Tolka Est. Rd. 11	23	J4
Tolka Quay 1	45	O8
Tolka Quay Rd. 1	62	P8
Tolka Rd. 3	36	L6
Tolka Vale 11	22	H4
Tolka Valley Rd. 11	21	F4
Tolka Vw. Ter. 11	22	H4
Tom Clarke Ho. 3	36	M6
Tom Kelly Rd. 2	49	K11
Tonduff Clo. 12	52	C14
Lugnaquilla Av.		
Tonguefield Rd. 12	48	G12
Tonlegee Av. 5	27	R2
Tonlegee Dr. 5	26	Q2
Tonlegee Rd. 5	26	Q2
Torlogh Gdns. 3	36	M6
Torlogh Par. 3	36	M5
Tourmakeady Rd. 9	24	L3
Tower Av. 6	49	K13
Tower Vw. Cotts. 11	35	J5
Townsend St. 2	44	L9
Trafalgar La., D.L.	59	S15
Trafalgar Ter., D.L.	59	S15
Tram Ter. 3	38	Q7
Tramway Ter. 4	51	O11
Tramway Ter. 3	35	J6
Station Rd.		
Tramway Ct., Sutton	29	W2
Tramway Vills. 6	48	H13
Tranquility Gro. 5	25	O2
Trees Av., Stillorgan	58	P16
Trees Rd., Stillorgan	57	O16
Trevor Ter. 2	44	M9
Grattan St.		
Trimleston Av., Booterstown	63	P13
Trimleston Dr., Stillorgan	63	P13
Trimleston Gdns., Stillorgan	63	P13
Trimleston Pk., Stillorgan	63	P13
Trimleston Rd., Stillorgan	63	P13
Trinity Coll. 2	44	L9
Trinity St. 2	43	K9
Trinity Ter. 3	36	M6
Tritonville Av. 4	45	O10
Tritonville Ct. 4	45	O10
Tritonville Cres. 4	45	O10
Tritonville Rd. 4	45	N10
Trycennell Pk. 8	41	E10
Tuckett's La., Howth	31	AA3
Tudor Rd. 6	50	L13
Turnberry, Howth	29	V2
Turrets, The 4	45	N10
Turrets Flats 6	49	K12
Rathmines Rd. Upper		
Tuscany Downs 5	27	R3
Tuscany Pk., Baldoyle	29	V2
Tymon Castle, Tallaght	52	D15
Tymon La., Tallaght	52	C14
Tymon N. Av., Tallaght	52	C14
Tymon N. Gdns., Tallaght	52	C15
Tymon N. Grn., Tallaght	52	C15
Tymon N. Gro., Tallaght	52	C15
Tymon N. Lawn, Tallaght	52	C15
Tymon N. Pk., Tallaght	52	C15
Tymon N. Rd., Tallaght	52	C15
Tymonville Av., Tallaght	52	D15
Tymonville Ct., Tallaght	52	C15
Tymonville Cres., Tallaght	52	C15
Tymonville Dr., Tallaght	52	C15
Tymonville Gro., Tallaght	52	C15
Tymonville Pk., Tallaght	52	C15
Tymonville Rd., Tallaght	52	C15
Tyrconnell Rd. 8	41	E10
Tyrconnell St. 8	41	E10
Tyrconnell Vills. 8	41	E9
Grattan Cres.		
Tyrone Pl. 8	41	E10

U

Name	Page	Grid
U.S.A. Embassy 8	32	D7
Ulster St. 7	35	J6
University Coll. 2	43	K10
Upper Cliff Rd., Howth	31	BB3
Upper Glen Rd., Castleknock	32	C7
Uppercross Rd. 8	42	G10
Usher St. 8	43	J9
Ushers Island 8	42	H8
Ushers Quay 8	43	J9

V

Name	Page	Grid
Valentia Par. 7	35	K7
Valentia Rd. 9	24	L4
Valeview Cres. 11	22	G4
Valeview Dr. 11	21	F4
Valeview Gdns. 11	21	F4
Valley Pk. Av. 11	21	E4
Valley Pk. Dr. 11	21	E4
Valley Pk. Rd. 11	21	E4
Vauxhall Av. 8	42	H10
Vavasour Sq. 4	45	N10
Venetian Hall 5	26	P4
Ventry Dr. 7	34	G5
Ventry Pk. 7	34	G5
Ventry Rd. 7	34	G5
Verbena Av., Kilbarrack	28	U3
Verbena Gro., Kilbarrack	28	U2
Verbena Pk., Kilbarrack	28	U2
Vergemount 6	50	M13
Clonskeagh Rd.		
Vergemount Hall 6	50	M13
Vergemount Isolation Hosp. 6	50	M13
Vergemount Pk. 6	50	M12
Vernon Av. (Clontarf) 3	38	Q7
Vernon Av. 6	49	K13
Frankfort Av.		
Vernon Ct. 3	38	Q7
Vernon Dr. 3	38	Q5
Vernon Gdns. 3	38	Q6
Vernon Gro. 3	38	Q6
Vernon Gro. (Rathgar) 6	49	K13
Vernon Heath 3	38	Q5
Vernon Par. 3	37	O6
Vernon Pk. 3	38	Q6
Vernon Ri. 3	38	Q5
Vernon St. 8	43	J10
Vernon Ter. 6	49	K13
Frankfort Av.		
Veronica Ter. 4	45	N9
Verschoyle Ct. 2	44	M10
Verschoyle Pl.		
Verschoyle Pl. 2	44	M10
Vesey Ms., D.L.	60	U16
Vesey Pl., D.L.	60	U16
Vicar St. 8	43	J9
Victoria Av. 4	50	M12
Victoria Quay 8	42	H8
Victoria Rd. (Clontarf) 3	37	O6
Victoria Rd. (Terenure) 6	55	J14
Victoria St. 8	43	J10
Victoria Ter. 3	38	Q7
Clontarf Rd.		
Victoria Ter. 14	56	M16
Victoria Ter., D.L.	61	V16
Victoria Vills. 3	37	N6
Malahide Rd.		
Victoria Vills. (Rathgar) 6	49	J13
Viking Pl. 7	42	H8
Arbour Hill		

Street	Page	Grid
Viking Rd. 7	42	H8
Villa Pk. Av. 7 (Ascal Pairc An Bhailtini)	33	F6
Villa Pk. Dr. 7 (Ceide Pairc An Bhailtini)	33	F6
Villa Pk. Gdns. 7 (Gardini Pairc An Bhailtini)	33	F6
Villa Pk. Rd. 7 (Bothar Pairc An Bhailtini)	33	F6
Village, The 5	27	S4
Village, The 9	24	L4
Village Ct. 14	54	H15
Villarea Pk., D.L.	61	W17
Villiers Rd. 6	49	K13
Vincent St. 8	43	J10
Vincent Ter. 9	35	K5
Violet Hill Dr. 11	22	H4
Violet Hill Pk. 11	22	H4
Violet Hill Rd. 11	22	H4
Virginia Dr. 11	21	F3
Virginia Pk.		
Virginia Pk. 11	21	F3
W		
Wad Bri. 9	23	K3
Wadelai Grn. 11	23	K3
Wadelai Rd. 11	23	J3
Wades Av. 5	27	R4
Wainsfort Av. 6	53	F14
Wainsfort Cres. 6	53	F14
Wainsfort Dr. 6	48	G13
Wainsfort Gdns. 6	53	F14
Wainsfort Cres.		
Wainsfort Gro. 6	54	G14
Wainsfort Pk. 6	54	G14
Wainsfort Rd. 6	53	F14
Waldemar Ter. 14	56	L16
Waldrons Bri. 14	55	K14
Walk, The 12	53	F15
Walkinstown Av. 12	46	D12
Walkinstown Cres. 12	46	D12
Walkinstown Dr. 12	46	D12
Walkinstown Grn. 12	46	D12
Walkinstown Par. 12	46	D12
Walkinstown Pk. 12	46	D12
Walkinstown Rd. 12 (Bothar Chille Na Manac)	46	D12
Wallace Rd. 12	47	E12
Walnut Av. 9	24	L4
Walnut Ct. 9	24	L4
Walnut Lawn 9	24	L4
Walnut Pk. 9	24	L4
Walnut Ri. 9	24	L4
Walsh Rd. 9	35	K5
Waltham Ter., D.L.	58	Q15
Walworth Rd. 8	43	J10
Victoria St.		
Wards Hill 8	43	J10
Warners La. 6	50	L11
Warren St. 8	49	K11
Warrenhouse Rd., Baldoyle	29	W2
Warrenmount 8	43	J10
Warrenmount Pl. 8	43	J10
Warrenpoint 3	37	O6
Warrington La. 2	44	M10
Warrington Pl.		
Warrington Pl. 2	44	M10
Warwick Ter. 6	50	L11
Sallymount Av.		
Wasdale Gro. 6	55	J14
Wasdale Pk. 6	55	J14
Washington La. 14	54	G16
Washington Pk. 14	54	G15
Washington St. 8	43	J10
Waterfall Av. 3	36	L6
Waterfall Rd. 5	27	R4
Waterloo Av. 3	36	M7
Waterloo La. 4	50	L11
Waterloo Rd. 4	50	M11
Watermill Av. 5	27	R4
Watermill Dr. 5	27	R4
Watermill Lawn 5	27	S4
Watermill Pk. 5	27	R4
Watermill Rd. (Bothar An Easa) 5	27	R4
Watling St. 8	42	H9
Waverley Av. 3	36	M6
Waverley Ter. 6	49	J12
Kenilworth Rd.		
Weavers La. 7	35	J7
Phibsborough Rd.		
Weavers Sq. 8	43	J10
Wellesley Pl. 1	36	L7
North Circular Rd.		
Wellington La. 4	50	M11
Wellington La. 12	53	E14
Wellington Monument 8	42	G8
Wellington Pk. 12	53	E14
Wellington Pl. (Donnybrook) 4	50	M11
Wellington Pl. N. 7	35	K7
Wellington Quay 2	43	K9
Wellington Rd. 4	50	M11
Wellington Rd. 8	41	F8
Wellington St. 7	35	K7
Wellington St., D.L.	60	U16
Wellmount Av. 11	21	F3
Wellmount Ct. 11	21	F3
Wellmount Cres. 11	21	F3
Wellmount Dr. 11	21	F3
Wellmount Grn. 11	21	F3
Wellmount Par. 11	22	G3
Wellmount Pk. 11	21	F3
Wellmount Rd. 11	21	F3
Wellpark Av. 9	36	L5
Wentworth Ter. 2	44	M9
Hogan Pl.		
Werburgh St. 8	43	J9
Wesley Pl. 8	49	J11
Wesley Rd. 6	49	J13
West Oil Jetty 1	62	P9
West Pk. 5	26	Q3
West Pk. Dr. 11	23	J4
West Rd. 3	36	M7
West Ter. 8	41	E9
Westbourne Rd. 6	54	H14
Westbrook 12	47	F13
Westbrook Rd. 14	56	L15
Westcourt 8	42	H9
Basin St. Upper		
Westcourt La. 8	42	H9
Western Rd. 8	42	H9
Western Way 7	35	J7
Westfield Rd. 6	48	H12
Westhampton Pl. 6	48	H13
Westland Ct. 2	44	L9
Cumberland St. S.		
Westland Row 2	44	L9
Westmoreland Pk. 6	50	L11
Westmoreland St. 2	43	K9
Weston Av. 14	56	L16
Weston Clo. 14	56	L16
Weston Gro. 14	56	L16
Weston Pk. 14	56	L16
Weston Rd. 14	56	L16
Weston Ter. 14	56	L16
Westwood Av. 11	21	E3
Westwood Rd. 11	21	E3
Wexford St. 2	43	K10
Wharton Ter. 6	49	J11
Harolds Cross Rd.		
White Oaks 14	56	M14
Whitebank Rd. 4	62	P9
Whitebarn Rd. 14	55	K15
Whitebeam Av. 14	50	M13
Whitebeam Rd. 14	50	M13
Whitechurch Abbey 14	54	H16
Whitechurch Rd. 14	54	H16
Whitefriar Pl. 8	43	K9
Aungier St.		
Whitefriar St. 8	43	K9
Whitehall Clo. 12	53	E14
Whitehall Gdns. 12	47	F13
Whitehall Pk. 12	53	E14
Whitehall Rd. (Rathfarnham) 14	55	K16
Whitehall Rd. E. 12	53	E14
Whitehall Rd. W. 12	53	E14
Whites La. N. 7	35	J7
Whitethorn Av. 5	25	O3
Whitethorn Clo. 5	25	N4
Whitethorn Cres. 5	25	O3
Whitethorn Gro. 5	25	O3
Whitethorn La. 4	45	N9
Thorncastle St.		
Whitethorn Pk. 5	25	O3
Whitethorn Ri. 5	25	O4
Whitethorn Rd. 5	25	N3
Whitethorn Rd. 14	50	M13
Whitton Rd. 6	48	H13
Whitworth Av. 3	35	K6
Whitworth Pl.		
Whitworth Pl. 3	35	K6
Whitworth Rd. 1	44	M8
Seville Pl.		
Whitworth Rd. 9	35	J6
Wicklow La. 2	43	K9
Wicklow St.		
Wicklow St. 2	43	K9
Wigan Rd. 9	35	K6
Wilderwood Gro. 12	53	E15
Wilfield 4	51	O11
Wilfield Rd. 4	51	O11
Willbrook Gro. 14	54	H16
Willbrook Lawn 14	54	H16
Willbrook Pk. 14	54	H16
Willbrook Rd. 14	54	H16
Willbrook St. 14	54	H16
Willfield Pk. 4	51	O11
Willfield Rd. 4	51	O11
William St. N. 1	36	L7
William St. S. 2	43	K9
William's La. 1	43	K8
Princes St. N.		
William's Pk. 6	49	K11
William's Pl. S. 8	43	J10
William's Pl. Upper 1	35	K6
William's Row 1	43	K8
Abbey St. Middle		
Willington Av. 12	53	E14
Willington Ct. 12	53	E14
Willington Cres., Tallaght	53	E15
Willington Dr. 12	53	E15
Willington Grn. 12	53	E15
Willington Gro. 12	53	E15
Willington Pk. 12	53	E15
Willington Gro.		
Willmont Av., D.L.	61	W17
Willow Bk., D.L.	60	U16
Willow Ms. 4	45	P12
Willow Pk. Av. 11	23	J2
Willow Pk. Clo. 11	23	J2
Willow Pk. Cres. 11	22	H2
Willow Pk. Dr. 11	23	J2
Willow Pk. Gro. 11	23	J2
Willow Pk. Lawn 11	23	J2
Willow Pk. Rd. 11	23	J2
Willow Pl., Booterstown	58	Q14
Willow Ter., Booterstown	58	Q14
Rock Rd.		
Willowbank Pk. 14	54	G16
Willowfield 4	51	O11
Willowfield Av. 14	57	N15
Willowfield Pk. 14	57	N15
Willows, The 11	34	H5
Willows, The, D.L.	60	T16
Wilson Cres., Stillorgan	57	O15
Wilson Rd., Stillorgan	57	O15
Wilsons Pl. 2	44	M9
Grants Row		
Wilton Pl. 2	44	L10
Wilton Ter. 2	44	L10
Windele Rd. 9	35	K5
Windgate Ri., Howth	31	BB4
Windgate Rd., Howth	31	BB4
Windmill Av. 12	47	F12
Windmill Cres. 12	47	F11
Windmill La. 2	44	M9
Windmill Pk. 12	47	F12
Windmill Rd. 12	47	F12
Windsor Av. 3	36	M6
Windsor Ct., D.L.	60	T17
Stradbrook Rd.		
Windsor Dr., D.L.	60	T17
Windsor Pk., D.L.	60	T17
Windsor Pl. 2	44	L10
Windsor Rd. 6	49	K12
Windsor Ter. 8	49	J
Windsor Ter., D.L.	61	V
Windsor Vills. 3	36	N
Winetavern St. 8	43	
Winton Av. 6	49	J
Winton Rd. 6	50	L
Wolfe Tone Av., D.L.	60	
Wolfe Tone Quay 7	42	H
Wolfe Tone St. 1	43	K
Wolseley St. 8	43	J
Wood Quay 8	43	
Wood St. 8	43	K
Woodbank Av. 11	21	E
Woodbank Dr. 11	21	E
Woodbine Av., Stillorgan	57	O
Woodbine Clo. 5	27	R
Woodbine Dr. 5	27	R
Woodbine Pk. 5	27	R
Woodbine Pk., Booterstown	63	P
Woodbine Rd. 4	51	O
Woodbine Rd. 5	27	S
Woodbine Rd., Stillorgan	51	O
Woodbine Ter. 14	56	M
Woodbrook Pk. 14	53	F
Woodcliff Hts., Howth	31	BB
Woodfield Av. 10	41	E
Woodfield Pl. 10	41	E
Woodfield Av.		
Woodland Pk., Stillorgan	58	P
Woodland Vills. 6	50	L
Woodlands 6	55	J
Woodlands, The 14	55	J
Woodlands Av., Stillorgan	58	P
Woodlands Dr., Stillorgan	58	P
Woodlawn Cres. 14	56	L
Woodlawn Gro. 14	56	L
Woodlawn Pk. 14	56	L
Woodlawn Pk., D.L.	60	U
Woodlawn Ter. 14	56	L
Woodside 3	38	O
Woodside 14	55	J
Woodside Dr. 14	55	J
Woodside Gro. 14	55	J
Woodstock Gdns. 6	50	L
Woodview Clo. 5	27	S
Woodview Cotts. 14	54	H
Woodview Pk. 5	27	S
Woodville Rd. 9	35	H
Botanic Av.		
Wynberg Pk., D.L.	59	S
Wynnefield Rd. 6	49	K
Wynnsward Dr. 14	56	M
Wynnsward Pk. 14	56	M
X		
Xavier Av. 3	36	M
Y		
Yale 14	57	N
Yankee Ter., D.L.	59	R
Yellow Rd. 9	24	M
Yewland Ter. 6	48	H
York Av. 6	49	K
York Rd. 4	45	N
York Rd. 6	49	K
York Rd., D.L.	60	U
York St. 2	43	K
York Ter., D.L.	60	U
Z		
Zion Rd. 6	55	J
Zoo Rd 8	42	
Zoological Gdns. 8	33	